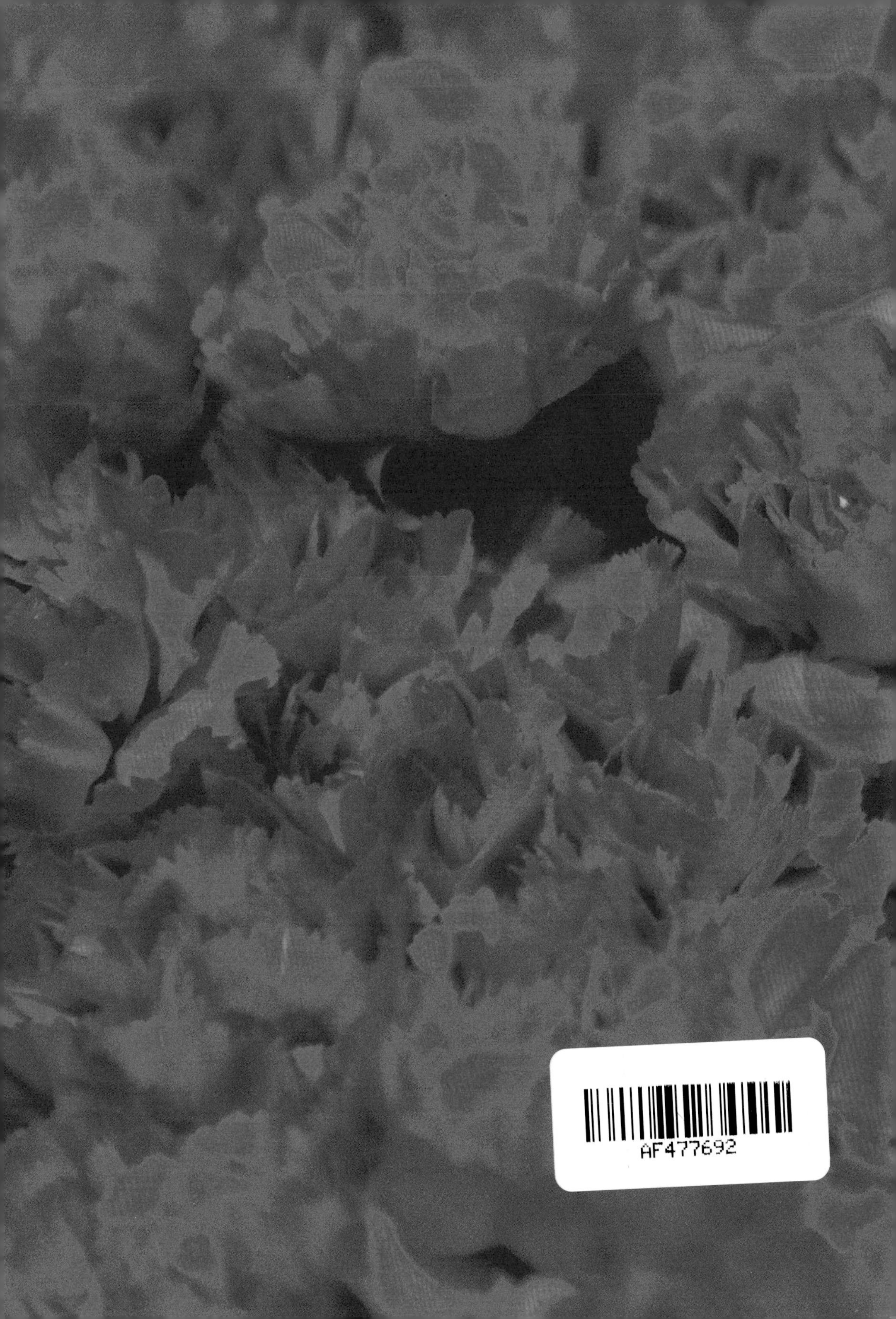
AF477692

KARYN OLIVIER

EVERYTHING THAT'S ALIVE MOVES

Institute of
Contemporary Art
University of Pennsylvania

Contents

Introduction

The exhibition *Everything That's Alive Moves,* opened at ICA in January of 2020.

At that time Karyn's powerful and monumental works spoke to history, something we did not realize was so close to us. The power of Karyn's installation stood testament to the emergence of this turbulent year, and its voice continues to resonate with us now.

As the Interim Daniel W. Dietrich, ll Director of ICA, it was a joy and an honor to work with Karyn and I am indebted to Anthony Elms, our Daniel and Brett Sundheim Chief Curator, for organizing the exhibition. I wish to acknowledge their incredible patience and understanding as we navigated the pandemic and were forced to close the exhibition to the public in March. While the museum was saddened to cancel the related programs, including poet, writer, and dancer Harmony Holiday's scheduled procession, we were enthralled by Holiday's translation of their original idea into an online film and suite of writings entitled *Until That Morning Comes.* Despite the early closure, we were thrilled to have had so many in-person and virtual visitors to the exhibition and programs. We are pleased the exhibition will have another audience as it travels to the University at Buffalo Art Galleries, guided by curator Liz Park. And in seeing both exhibitions captured in this beautiful book, we thank Sonia Yoon and Andrianna Campbell-LaFleur for their attentiveness and care.

At ICA, this exhibition would not have been possible without the support and leadership of our peerless staff. I want to acknowledge our Marc J. Leder Director of Curatorial Affairs, Robert Chaney, our Registrar Kate Abercrombie—who was particularly integral to procuring the necessary fresh carnations for *May 12, 1985—*

and Curatorial Administrative Coordinator Caitlin Palmer. The exhibition required much structural, mechanical, and construction expertise, and these unknowns were beautifully answered by the installation crew under the guidance of Chief Preparator & Building Administrator Paul Swenbeck. Additional thanks to our Director of Development Bruno Nouril as well as our Director of Marketing & Communications Jill Katz, and everyone at ICA who contributed to the exhibition including our full staff, docents, work-study students, and supporters. Special thanks are also due to DAJ Director of Public Engagement James Britt, Visitor Services Coordinator Elizabeth Chong, and the front desk attendants who gracefully and deftly made Karyn's work *May 12, 1985* possible.

External support for *Everything That's Alive Moves* was generously given by The Andy Warhol Foundation for the Visual Arts, the Edna Wright Andrade Fund of the Philadelphia Foundation, the Henry Moore Foundation, and by a Tyler Dean's Grant from Temple University. Individual support was provided by Nancy & Leonard Amoroso, Danielle Mandelbaum Anderman, Cecile & Christopher D'Amelio, Cheri & Steven Friedman, Christina Weiss Lurie, Josephine Magliocco, Lori & John Reinsberg, Patricia & Howard Silverstein, and by Stephanie & David Simon.

This exhibition would not have been possible without the leadership and support of our Board of Advisors, including Chair David Simon. At the University level, we are eternally grateful to both our President Amy Gutmann and our Provost Wendell Pritchett, who led us through this difficult and challenging year.

JOHN MCINERNEY

Interim Daniel W. Dietrich, ll Director, Institute of Contemporary Art
Executive Director, The Sachs Program for Arts Innovation
University of Pennsylvania

Moving the Obelisk
NOTES AND NARRATION

KARYN OLIVIER

Moving the Obelisk, 2019–2020
Cardboard, dirt, wood, tape, glue, hardware, and single-channel color video, sound
12 minutes
Courtesy of the artist and Tanya Bonakdar Gallery, New York / Los Angeles

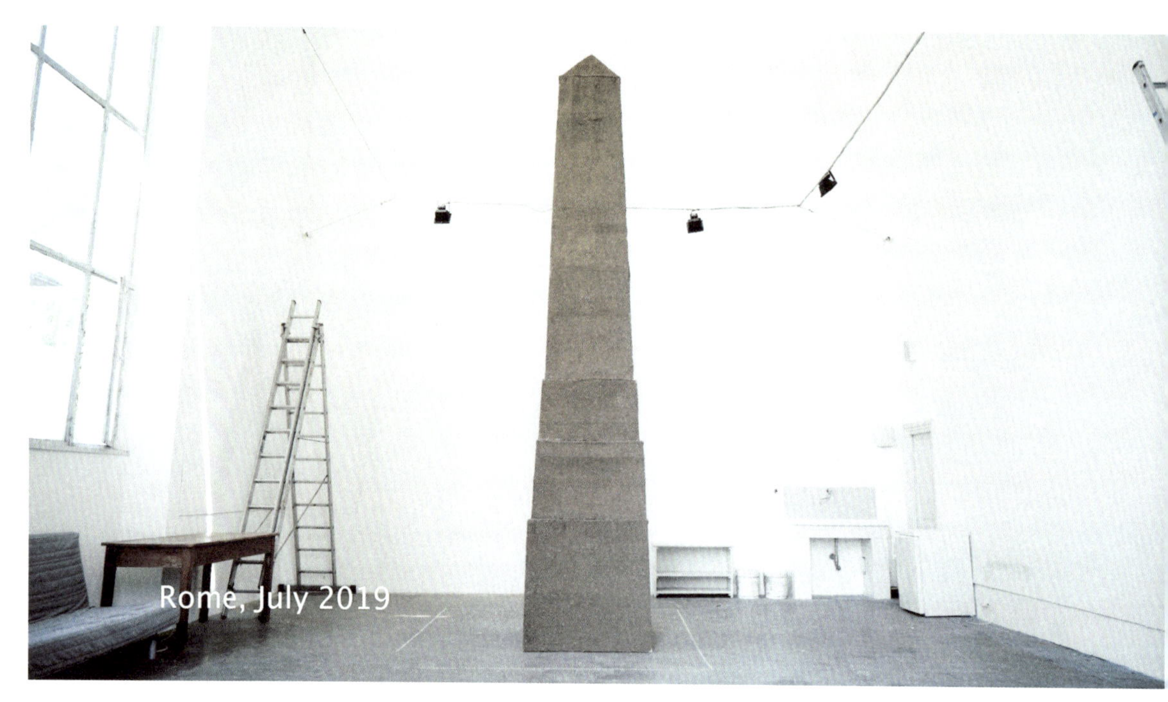

Rome, July 2019

(OVERVIEW)

"The past must address its present."

An obelisk. Comprised of a square, tapering shaft, and a pyramidion of 60 degrees at its top. Monolithic, excavated. Made from one solid stone: granite. The Greeks called them *obeliskos*, but the ancient Egyptian named them *Tekhen*, taken from the verb meaning "to pierce." They were guarantors of a pharaoh's existence in the afterlife. Piercing the sky, connecting the earth to the realm of the sun god. Immortal, imposing, larger than life. When we were kings and queens we had slaves.

And then the Romans came.

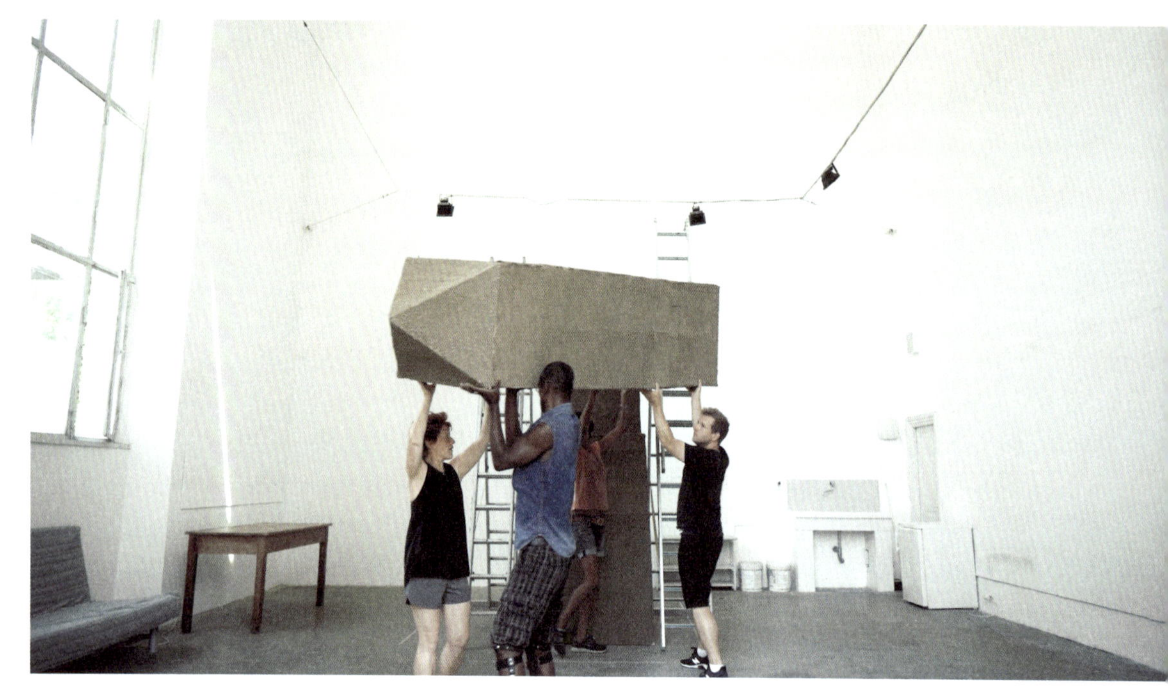

(TAKING IT DOWN)

It's common knowledge that Rome now has more erect obelisks than
anywhere else, including Egypt, homeland of the obelisk. These were
carved in one long, horizontal piece, from the bedrock of a quarry.
This obelisk, too, was made on site. Not quarried, but excavated
from the ground. Roman dirt, Roman soil. Dirt is in the foundation
of our buildings, the very infrastructure that surrounds us. Its use is
everywhere, dating back to prehistory—cob, adobe, rammed earth.
And here, a material that effortlessly links our past with the present.
"*Remember me*, whispers the dust."

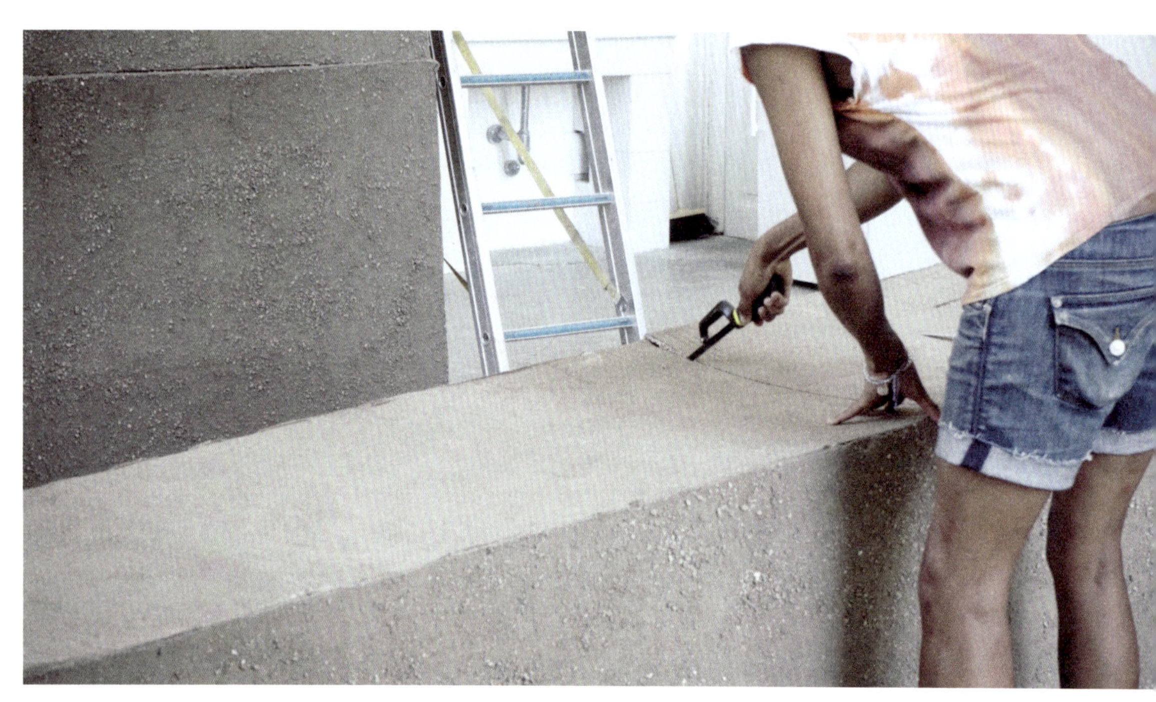

(CUTTING IT DOWN)

Most cardboard boxes are reincarnated as containers for goods to be shipped. Some escape this karma to serve a more urgent function—as a temporary shelter, a shield, a cot. The Egyptians were the original recyclers. Kings, in their hubris, demanded that previous signatures of power be chiseled away, removed. Off with the name of the old pharaoh, on with the new. Reworked obelisks, sphinxes claimed as their own. The Romans witnessed this and copied it, too.

This hollow shell is not really an obelisk, by definition. But what of the weight of emptiness? Its total weight, dispersed along its body, is probably close to my own. The cardboard, the dirt—similar in color. Similar to me in hue.

"Even the dirt keeps breathing a small breath."

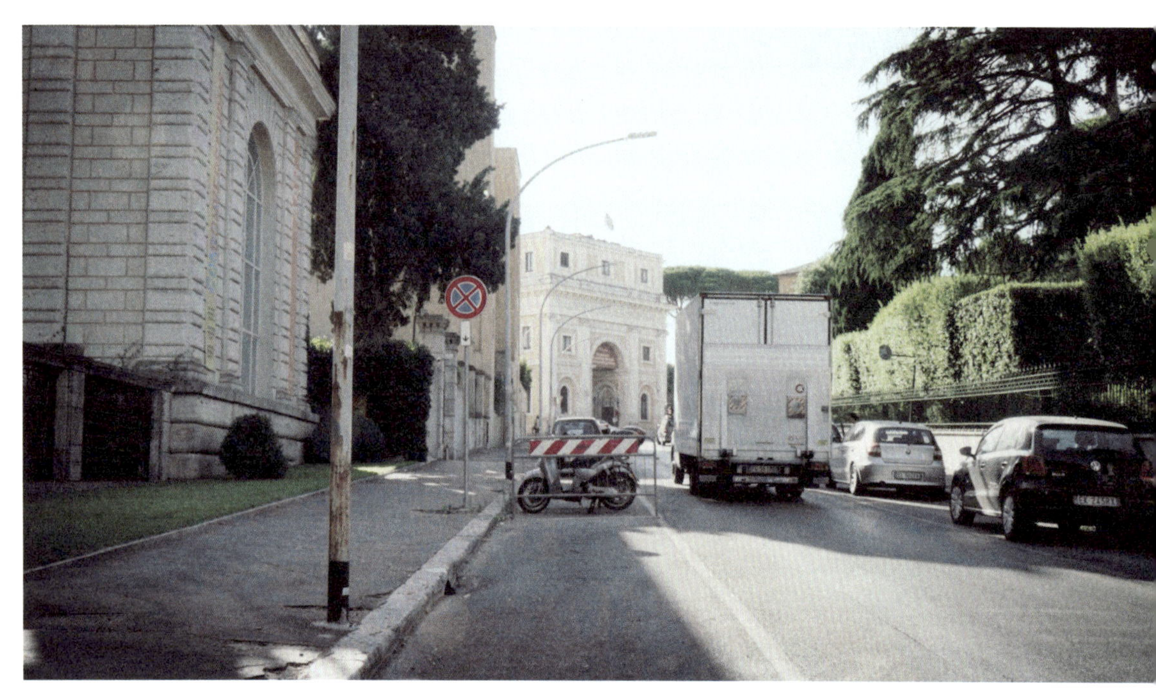

(CRATING AND DEPARTING)

What happens to a monument, whose very meaning is derived
by its stature—static, impervious, eternal, and timeless—when
compromised and surrendered?

How will it be defined in a new location? What will it mean when it
gets here from there? What has been left behind? What legacy is lost?

MEDITERRANEAN SEA

ATLANTIC OCEAN

(OCEANS)

Obelisks mined near the banks of the Nile traveled downriver to locations where they stood for millennia. Then they crossed the Mediterranean to the shores of Roman emperors as trophies of war. Forced movements. Trade routes. Power follows trade. This pillage—slaves, obelisks, sundials, exotica—destined to be paraded in the Roman Triumph.

Years later special ships would be outfitted to carry obelisks across the Atlantic to the New World. But not before the onslaught of European ships steered again by greed and conquest, outfitted to carry millions. "Nowhere else is the disorientation, violence and alienation of contemporary capitalism more manifest." "Water is an element which remembers the dead."

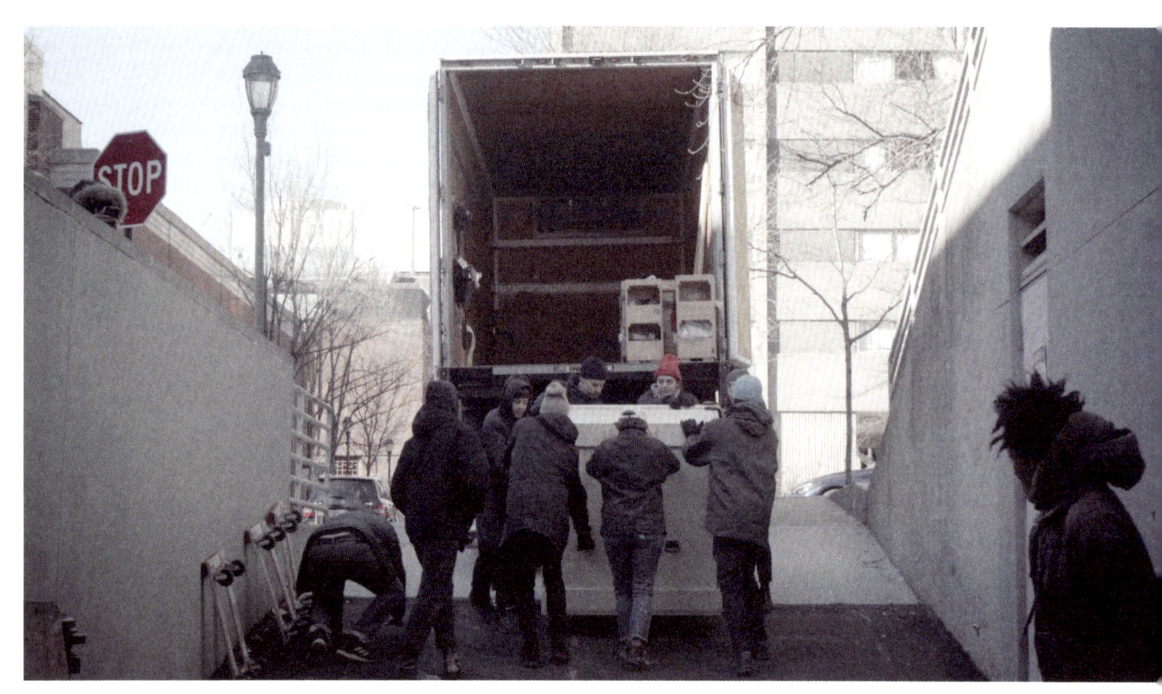

STOP

(ARRIVING IN PHILADELPHIA)

How were these massive objects made portable?

The stone, dragged from the quarry to a dry dock on the Nile, awaited
the season when the waters would rise, allowing the next leg of the
journey down river.

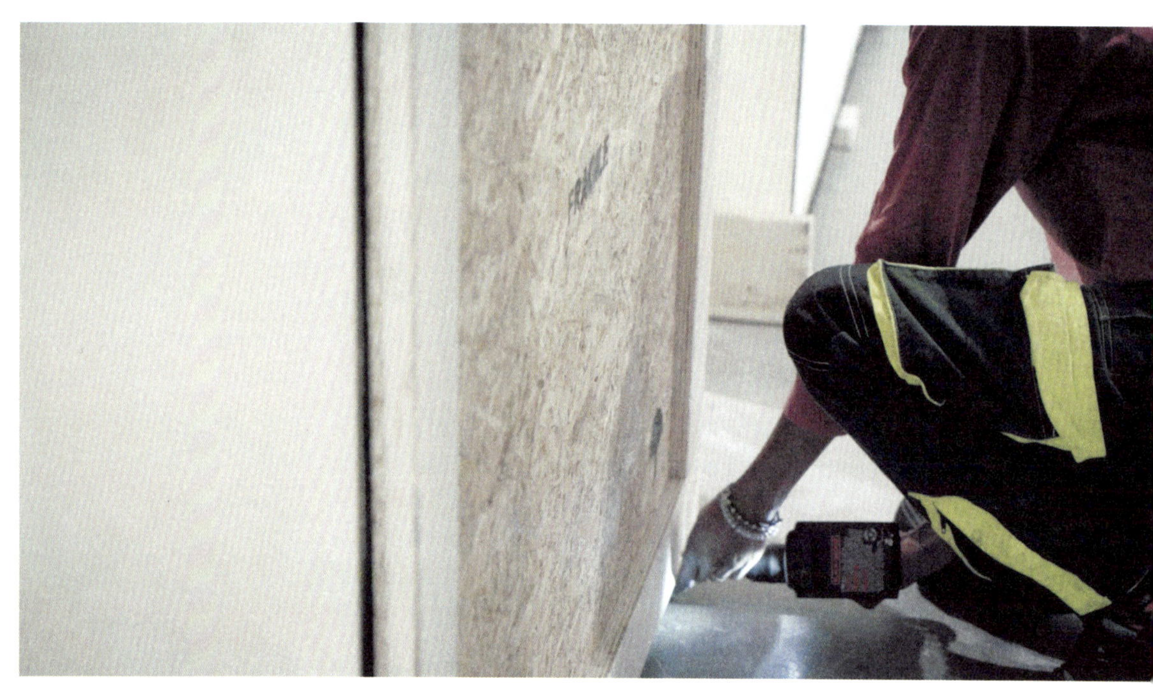
FRAGILE

(UNPACKING)

Sojourner Truth said, "When I left the house of bondage I left everything behind. I wanted to keep nothing of Egypt on me, and so I went to the Lord and asked him to give me a new name." Planted somewhere new. Reborn. How fitting that New York, the "Empire State," has one of three genuine Egyptian obelisks all misnamed Cleopatra's Needle, though they predate her reign by one thousand years. We think of her beauty but not of her slaves.

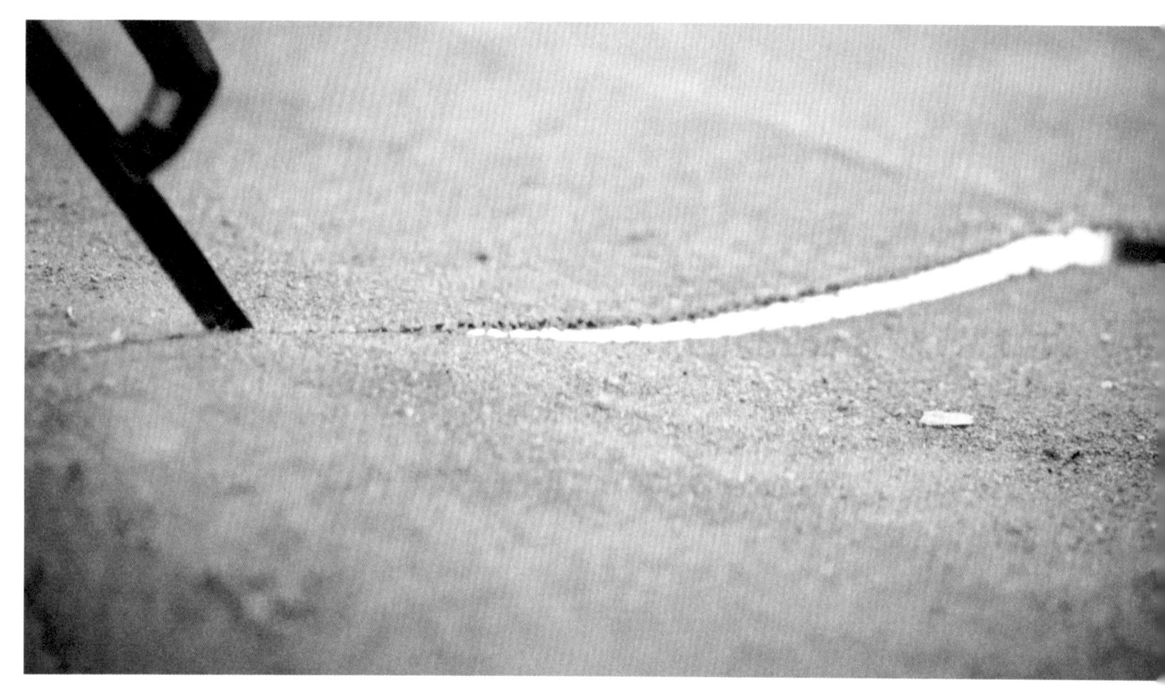

(CUTTING AND MENDING)

Slavery begins with civilization. There are two Egypts for us. Egypt the land of Hebrew bondage; Egypt—the Black Land, a magnificent African civilization, the realm of powerful rulers. "Which of the two Africas is in African-American?" In African-Caribbean? "Which Africa is ours?"

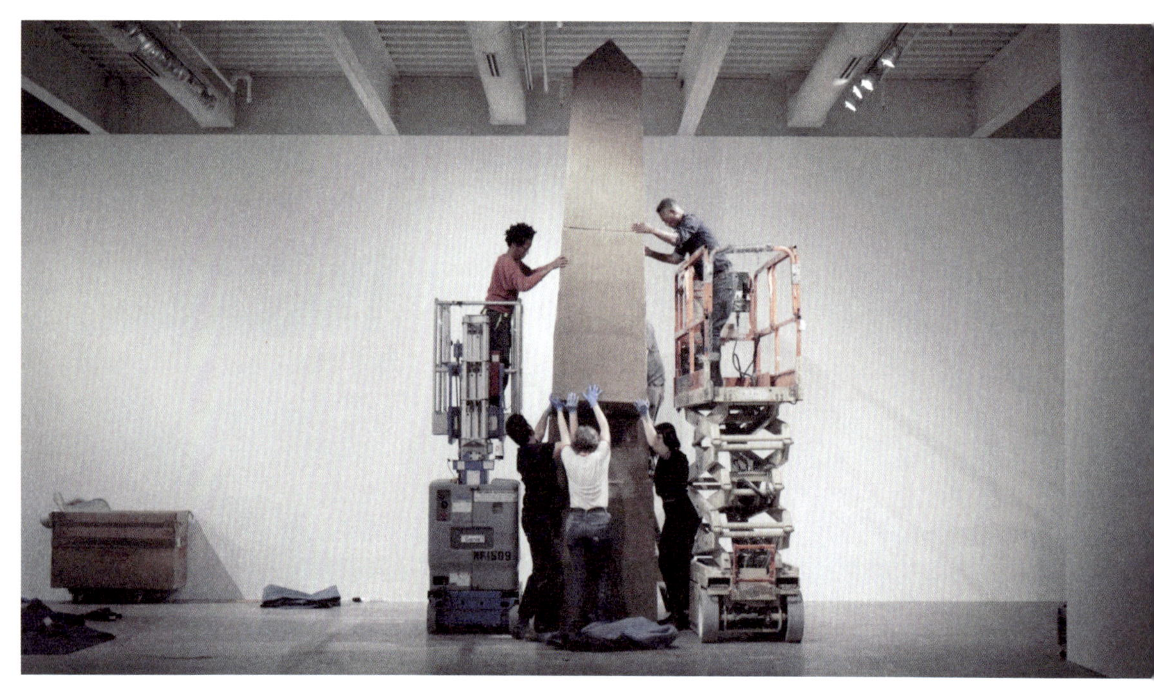

(RAISING IT)

We still don't know everything about how they did it, transitioning that
obelisk from the horizontal to the vertical. It's believed that as many
as fifty thousand men were needed to pull and drag these monuments.
Every part of an obelisk's journey was designed to be spectacular.

In ancient Egypt, there was the original Philadelphia, which means
"Brotherly Love" in Greek. The first World's Fair took place in our
Philadelphia in 1876. The entrance to the Egyptian court was flanked
by two towers, which mimicked the obelisks traditionally positioned
in front of the pharaoh's temple to Sun Ra. They were inscribed "The
oldest people of the world send its morning greeting to the youngest
nation."

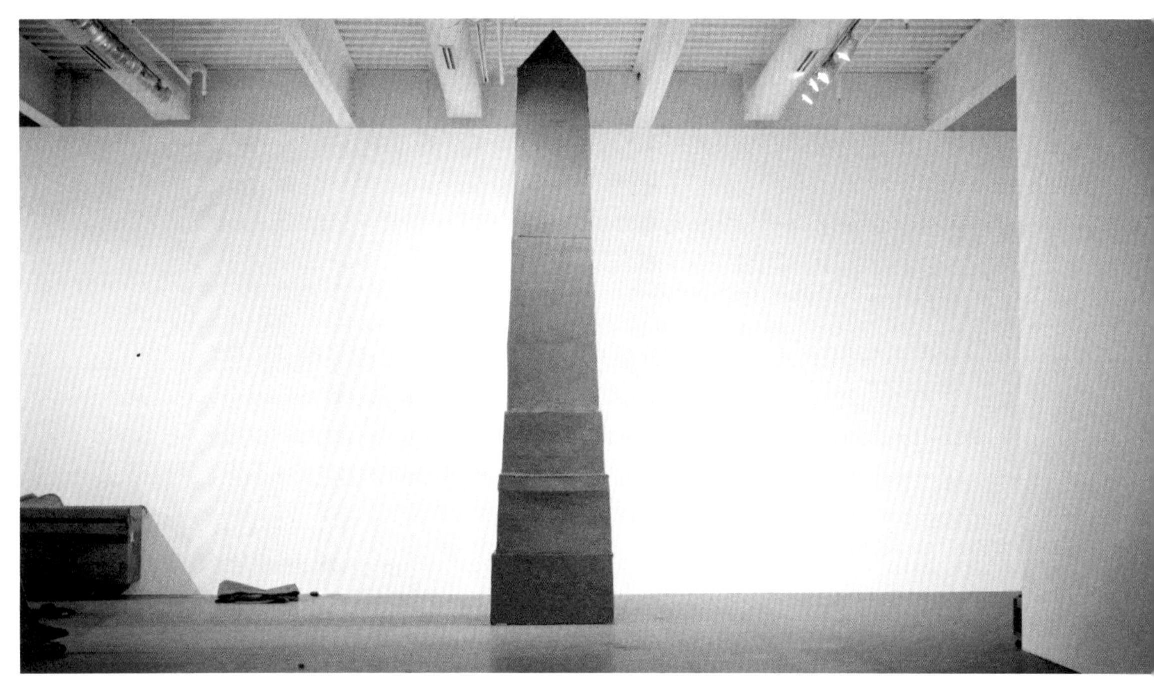

(ASSEMBLED)

A monument made. A monument dismantled. Dissected, mended,
put back together. A talisman, a spectacle. A form recreated from an
ancient Black culture, resituated in Philadelphia, "a Black city." And
now—at least temporarily—this fragile obelisk sits in close proximity
to its kin, the Sphinx of Ramses II, the largest in the Western
Hemisphere. It is wildly displaced, a stranger in a strange land.

"…the past does not exist independently from the present. Indeed,
the past is only past because there is a present, just as I can point
to something over there only because I am here. But nothing is
inherently over there or here… The past—or more accurately,
pastness—is a position."

QUOTES

"The past must address its present."
Nobel lecture by Wole Soyinka

"*Remember me*, whispers the dust."
"The Angels" by Peter Huchel

"Even the dirt kept breathing a small breath."
"Root Cellar" by Theodore Roethke

"Nowhere else is the disorientation, violence and alienation
of contemporary capitalism more manifest."
"The Forgotten Space" by Allan Sekula and Noël Burch

"Water is an element which remembers the dead."
"Water and Dreams: An Essay on the Imagination of Matter"
by Gaston Bachelard

"Which of the two Africas is in African-American? Which Africa is ours?"
"Lose Your Mother" by Saidiya Hartman

"…the past does not exist independently from the present. Indeed, the
past is only past because there is a present, just as I can point to something
over there only because I am here. But nothing is inherently over there
or here… The past—or more accurately, pastness—is a position."
"Silencing the Past" by Michel-Rolph Trouillot

Of Reverence and Revenants

ANTHONY ELMS

In 1985 there was quite a hullabaloo in Manhattan. An acrimonious fight was underway to determine the fate of sculptor Richard Serra's public commission for the Foley Federal Plaza. The work, *Tilted Arc*, was a 120-foot-long, twelve-foot-high curve made from the artist's familiar COR-TEN steel that bisected the plaza. Petitions from offended employees who worked in nearby buildings led to public hearings that led to a federal lawsuit that led to the eventual removal of the work in 1989. Nearly all arguments pro and con centered on aesthetics and democratic ideals—appealing either to a right not to be impeded in crossing federally funded public space, or a right to artistic expression. No matter to which side one's sympathies drifted, the accusations grew anything but respectful in tone. The interwoven power dynamics went sadly underdeveloped by and large, as self-regarding ideals alternated with small-minded ideals echoing far beyond the canyons of Lower Manhattan.

The tenor of that debate lingers for me more than any rusty detail about Serra and public art. A lingering drone that calls forth an unrelated fragment from poet Lisa Robertson as reminder, ". . . we're complicity's monuments / And the city is seriously quaint!"[1] I can't help but think that more feelings of complicity in the arguments might have created space for thinking about exactly what and who were sharing space. But no.

Returning midstream, 1985, predemolition, an opinionated dissent on *Tilted Arc* appeared in the *Village Voice*: "Debby with Monument," written by Gary Indiana, who was then daylighting as art critic. His assessment was tart, some say caustic. I say quite fair, and remarkable at the time for the broader landscape he charted: art's relationship to money and power, the rise of Reaganism and the rabid defunding of social programs, the scathing policies of our government, and the willful clash of egos amidst it all. Specifically, Indiana turned to the state of the homeless and marginalized, particularly those looking for green cards and those ejected from mental

1   Lisa Robertson, *Lisa Robertson's Magenta Soul Whip* (Toronto: Coach House Books, 2009), 87.

institutions, really any and all at the edges of citizenship as administered under federal laws—those for whom the buildings and space of the Foley Federal Plaza held consequence. If my diversion into a 1980s downtown New York public art fiasco is worth the time for an essay that considers Karyn Olivier's recent sculpture as memorial or monument in 2020, it is for an opportunity to think within the conclusion of Indiana's essay:

> Yet they [the homeless] define the space of public sculpture in a sense that a hunk of steel emanating from a drawing board in Richard Serra's office never could. They occupy real space, as distinct from the space of idealistic projections, utopian fantasies, and masturbatory empires. They are the brothers and sisters of the people huddled in the halls of the Jacob K. Javits Federal Building waiting to be photographed for immigration documents. They couldn't care less if Richard Serra's contract with the GSA is abrogated. Their contract with anything has been severed at the nerve by the government Richard Serra expects to do the proper democratic thing. That government has demonstrated, for the past five years, that it is capable of any deception, any illegality, capable indeed of anything. Compared to what it does every day to those ordinary people who can't understand modern art, knocking over some egomaniac's prefab sculpture is a hilarious canard. In case Richard Serra never heard this from anybody else, I'd like him to hear it from me: lie down with dogs, get up with fleas.[2]

Sinkingly familiar? Feels so from where I sit. *Tilted Arc* was public art, not monument or memorial. "But both monuments and public art can let us down, keeping us at a distance, failing to engage this massive captive audience in its line of sight," as Olivier has noted.[3]

2   Gary Indiana, "Debby with Monument," in *Vile Days* (South Pasadena: Semiotext(e), 2018), 58.

3   "Karyn Olivier and Paul Ramírez Jonas in Conversation," *Inbound: Houston* (Philadelphia: no publisher, 2015), 32.

Karyn has long been engaged with public art and public space even when in a gallery, and for *Everything That's Alive Moves* we considered three new and three existing sculptures with this in mind, rethinking publicness as a state of memorial or monument. Of immediate recognition when looking around the gallery was, rather than memorial or monument, the fact that every sculpture desired a location somewhere besides the indoors. An obelisk, a brick wall, a carousel, a car, ringing church bells, a flower: each spoke to an encounter or presence in the public sphere with bystanders and passersby and the compounded subjectivity of civic space. Still, in publicness Olivier's work rarely traffics in the reverence for proper nouns or specific events by which we tend to think of memorials or monuments. With this effect underlining, her materials read with broadly recognized categorizations: shoes, clothing, bricks, steel, car cover, cardboard, bell, red carnation. There's no alchemical change of base matter into gold and certainly no attempt at a sly preceptual game of handmade for machine made. Materials do not stand in for people or persons; they do not become persons or people. She thinks with the behavior of the objects in our social, political, perceptual world and recasts them in shifted roles. "For example, I understand this table. And now that I think I know this table, how can I change it?"[4] Materials are matters of behaviors.

To use the *Tilted Arc* fiasco as a landscape in which *Everything That's Alive Moves* is to say I'm uninterested in valorizing or demonizing either side of that controversy. Indiana's conclusion cuts through quaint questions of site-specific process and form, disregards guilt, and looks to where the work was built and who the work was built around, and how lines of influence and methods of engagement extend from commissioner through maker to viewer and subject. In this, we could sit and listen to Olivier's exhibition as it reverberated and echoed in an emotional space cultivated by

4   "Monumental Exchange 2: Sharon Hayes, Karyn Olivier, and Paul M. Farber," in
     Monument Lab: Creative Speculations for Philadelphia, ed. Paul M. Farber and Ken Lum
     (Philadelphia: Temple University Press, 2020), 267.

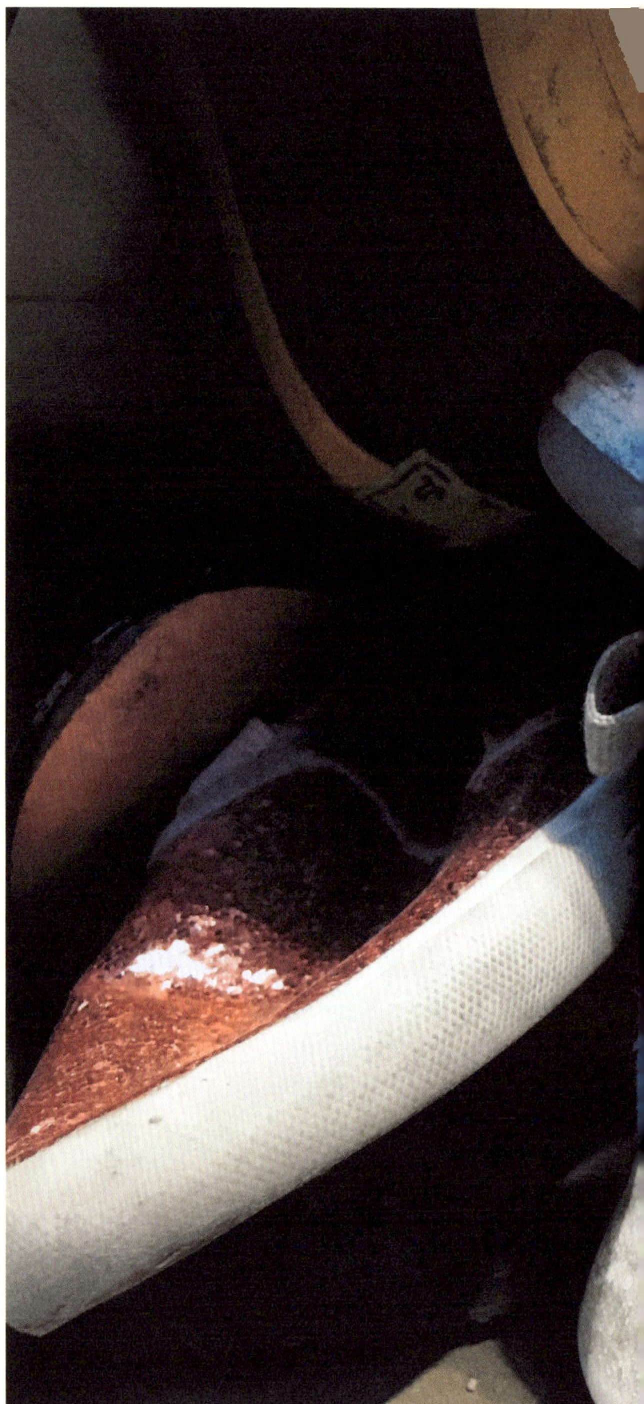

Car Cover and Export Shoes (detail), 2018
Car cover, expired shoes, and support
materials
15.5 × 6 × 4.5 ft.
Courtesy of the artist and Tanya Bonakdar
Gallery, New York / Los Angeles

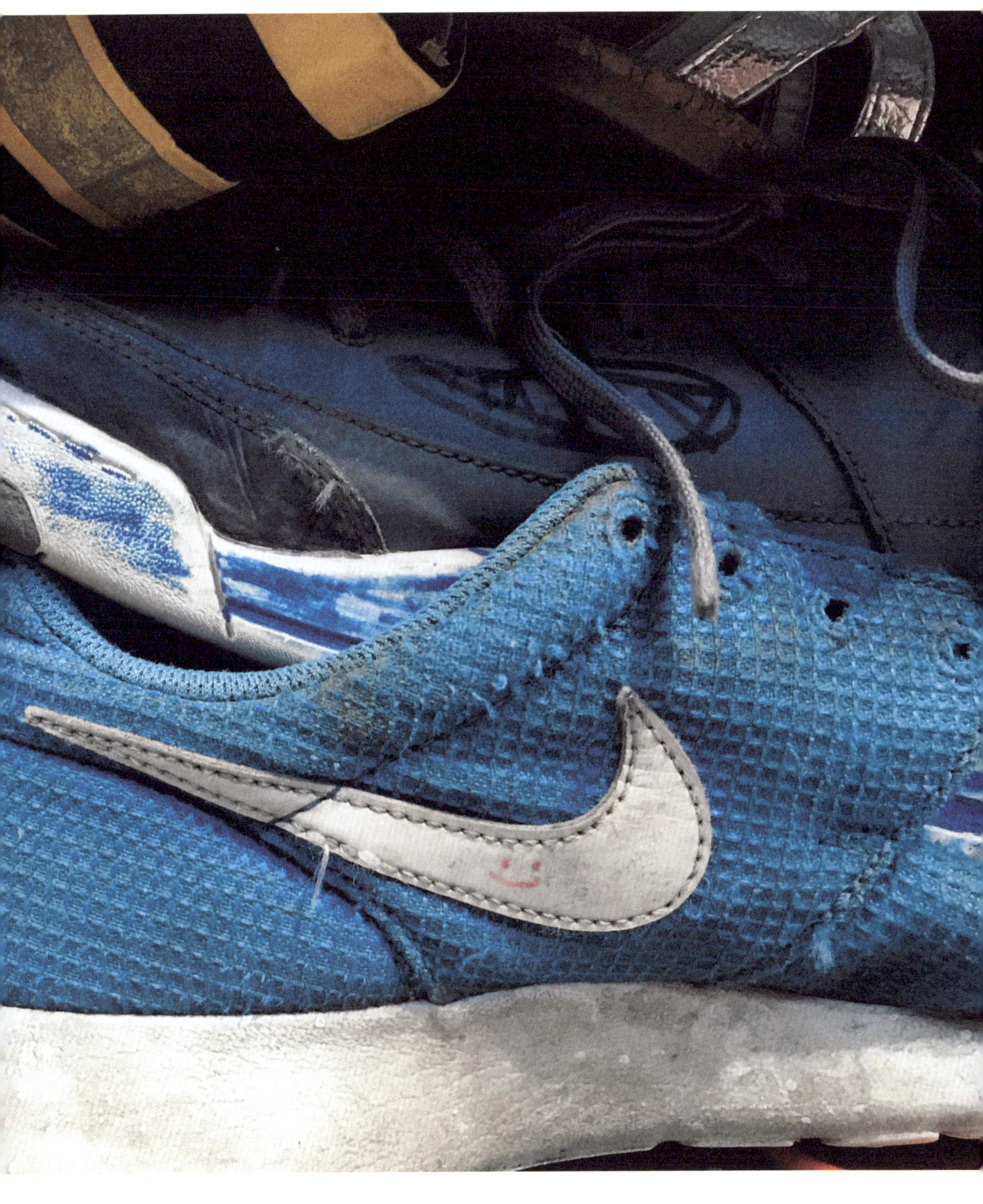

"Debby with Monument." Indiana's bitter resolution recognizes the contract of complicity that defines all of us relative citizenship, governance, and speech as soon as we enunciate or enact a connection with place. In this it is irrelevant if we think Serra in the right and the federal government in the wrong, or vice versa, or fall somewhere in between—we are always entangled within the brambles of this nation-state. Sitting with this feeling helps us recognize in Olivier's accumulated carousel, shoes, clothing, bricks, steel, car cover, cardboard, bells, and red carnations a reckoning with huddled individuals, abrogated contracts, severed nerves—as well as the real places we navigate when building any sense of beauty or justice, or pain, or little plot of space in proximity. In other words, the *we* around; daily presence as monument and memorial and material in change.

What's within this *we*? Definitely imperfection and negotiation. Many subjects in imbalance too as categorizations and definitions always fix to bodies and identifications. Olivier's recent thinking has revolved around civic spaces, specifically monuments and memorials. They approach plural forms of speech.

> Any subject is supported, spoken, and carried or disallowed
> and foreclosed by others, in a matrix of reciprocity,
> empathy, and power that conditions the very possibility
> of embodiment. As soon as she speaks and names,
> the political subject emerges. Her agency is a verbal
> one; architecture and governance can only interpret,
> fix or abstract the fluency of the linguistic given,

as Lisa Robertson might help guide with *Thresholds: A Prosody of Citizenship*.[5] And so it is in the shadows cast by monuments and memorials where we catch glimpses of political subjects emboldened by interpretive powers of architectures and governance. Olivier questions who these subjects are not and how that presumption can be questioned,

---

5   Lisa Robertson, *Thresholds: A Prosody of Citizenship* (London: Book Works and The Common Guild, 2018), 2–3.

driven in part by her planning, building, and writing for her recent commissions in the public sphere.

One such important public project, *The Battle Is Joined* (2017), temporarily surrounded the 1903 *Battle of Germantown Memorial* in Philadelphia's historic Vernon Park with a mirrored enclosure. For three months, rather than seeing the heroic stone monument to an important if ultimately unsuccessful Revolutionary War battle, Germantown residents saw their everyday selves reflected in acrylic. The shiny covering was not simply beautiful or cloaking; it was a way to refract the experience of the park, encouraging visitors to see it anew and to recall with a different emphasis, to revisit histories and forms overlooked through an entrenched familiarity that did not reflect the passersby who were now checking themselves out. The ever-changing beauty of Olivier's surface treatment to the past opened a hole in daily ambience. Speaking of *The Battle Is Joined*, the artist said:

> Maybe monuments can be instruments that offer us a
> mirror to give witness to ourselves, our community,
> our city, or to the world. Or maybe they implore us to
> be aware of the present moment and allow us to reflect
> on our shared complicated histories. It can be a space
> that interrogates our histories and poses questions
> about our past that can speak about its impact today.[6]

The Battle Is Joined remade the monument into the grounds, the people, and the incidental and barely registered movements of the setting. Locals considered their own mirror images and the disconnect from what was now covered. Looking with this attitude of reflection and questioning, Olivier's focus at ICA on revisiting and, in one case, expanding three earlier works, *It's Not Over 'Til It's Over* (2004), *Car Cover and Export Shoes* (2018), and *Fortified* (2018–2020, elsewhere titled *Wall*), in *Everything That's Alive Moves* set a new

6   "Monumental Exchange 2," 266.

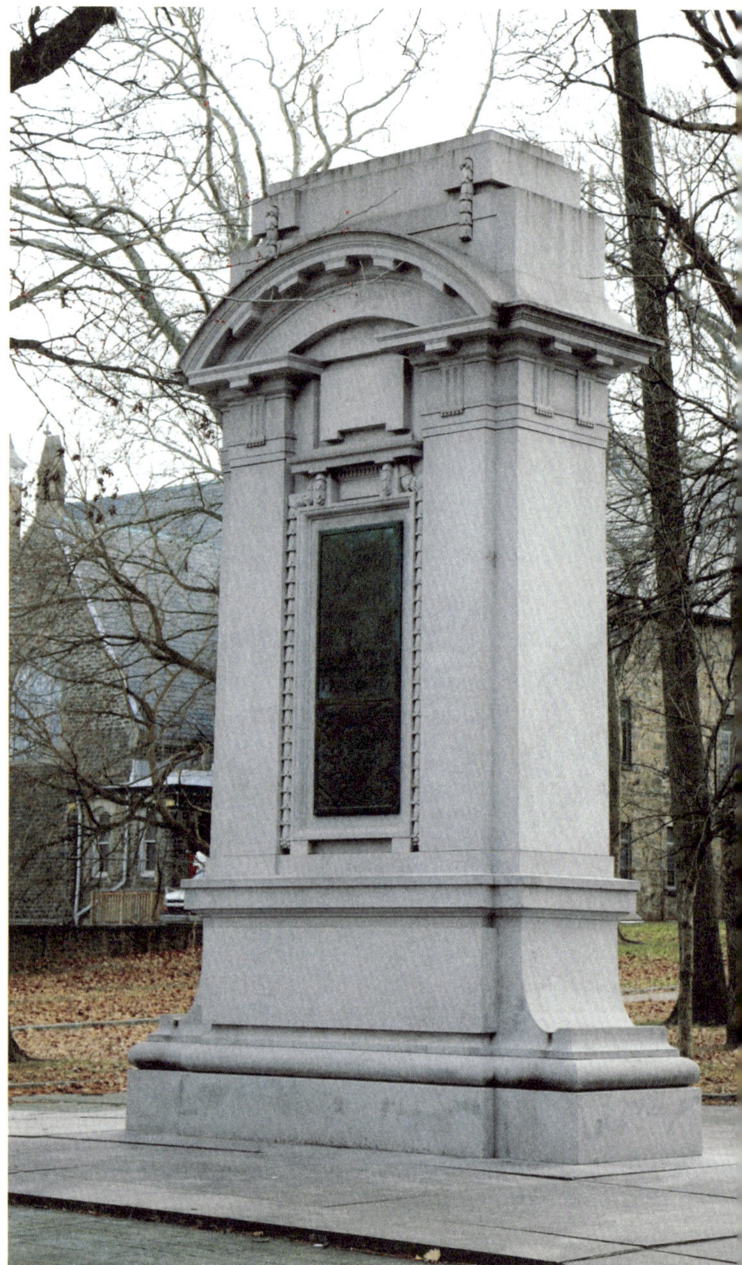

The Battle is Joined, 2017
Monument Lab, Mural Arts,
Vernon Park, Philadelphia
Mirrored acrylic, plywood, studs
14 × 20 × 5.5 ft.
Courtesy of the artist

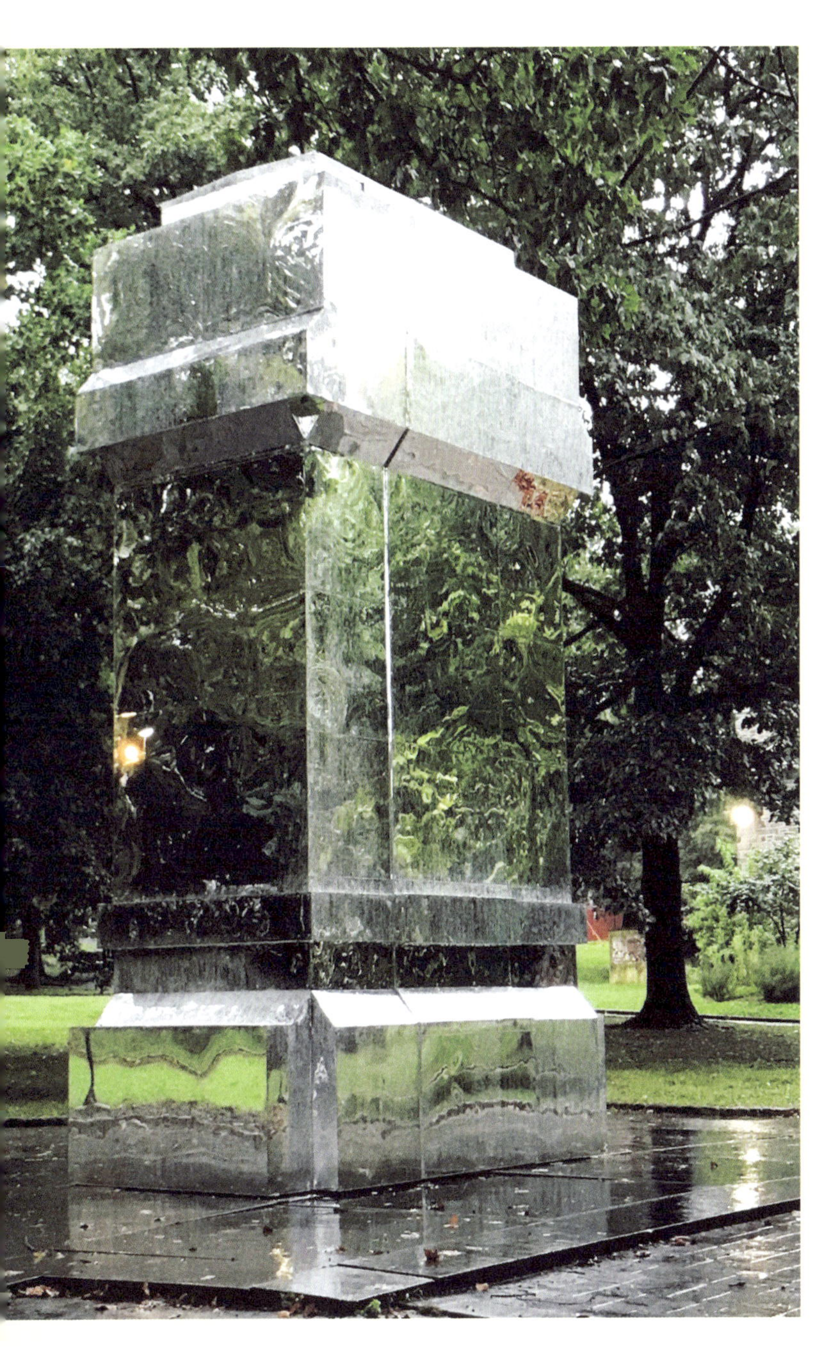

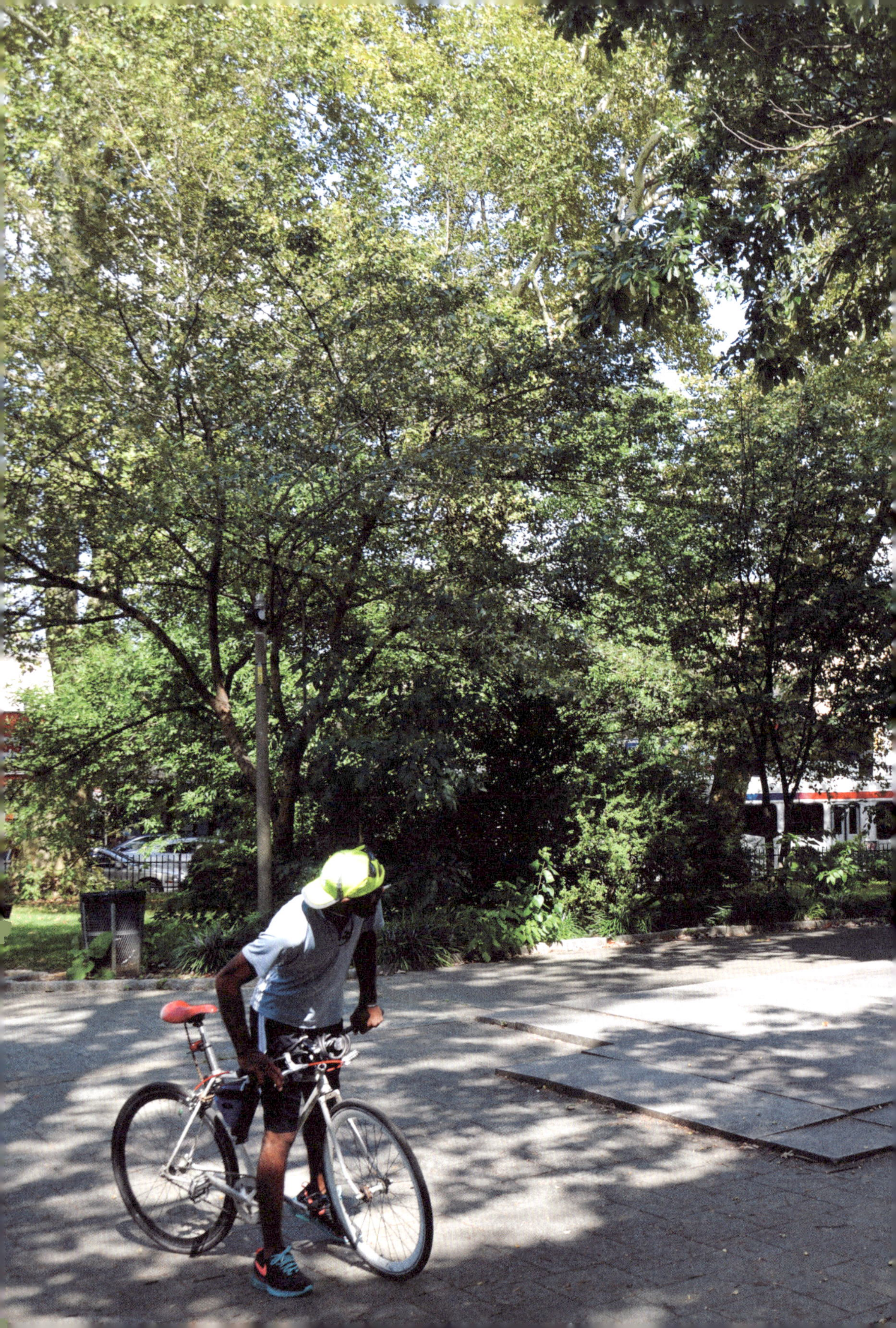

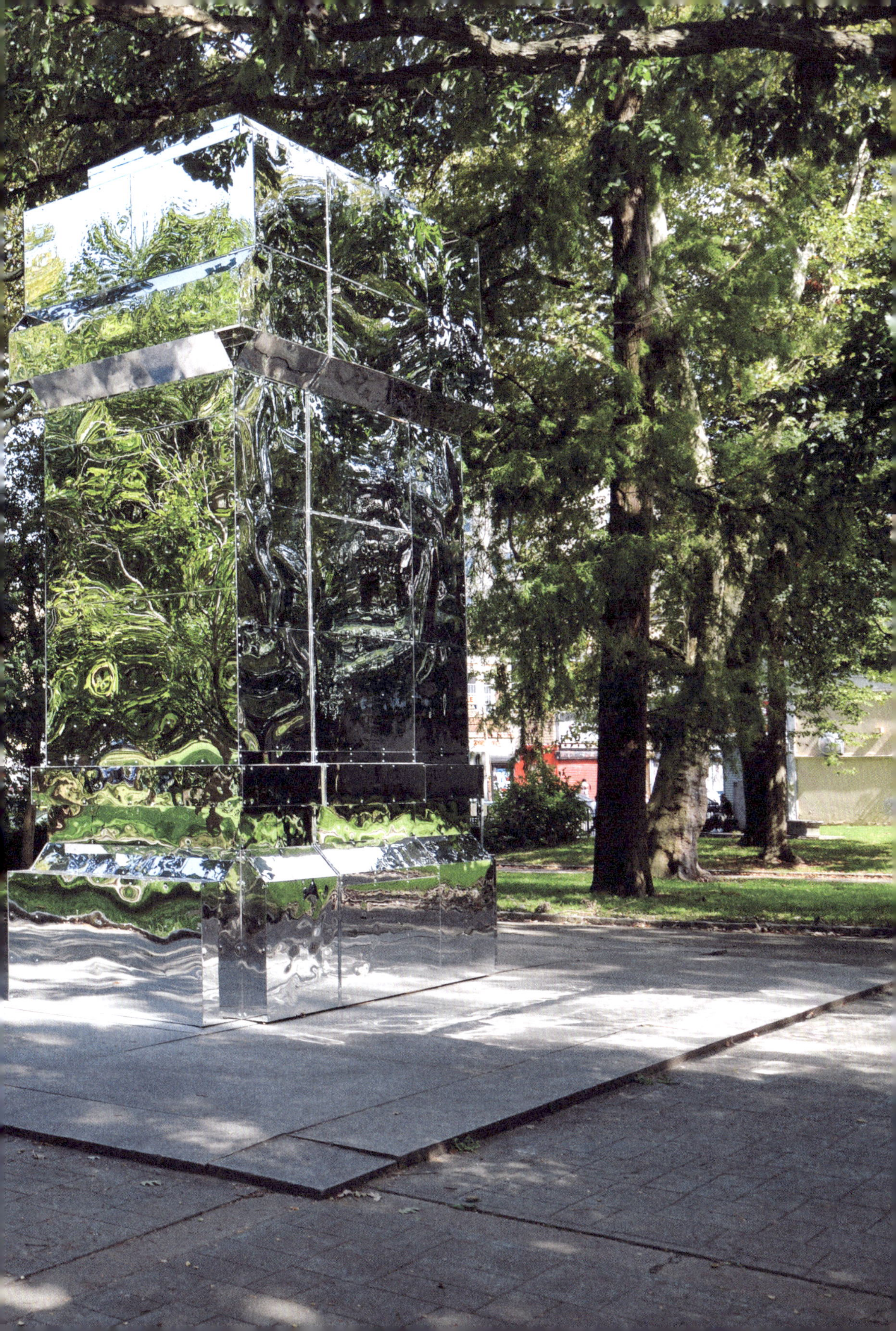

landscape in which to reconsider what her works honor or stage, looking at each as a site for mutable political subjects.

She explored the emotional impact of monuments and the political significance of memorials: how each in turn evokes and abstracts citizenship; how monuments and memorials fix belief in spaces of gathering; and how they alternately can speak in defense of or with suspicion toward a public, collective voice. Which side of *Fortified* are you on and do you find yourself safe or cut off? Where and why were shoes diverted and gathered to form a car? What is a carousel that offers seating for only one? The sculptures are undeniably Olivier's, still in the accumulation of labor, brick, clothing, shoes (*Fortified* and *Car Cover and Export Shoes*), and even in accumulating time (*It's Not Over 'Til It's Over*), within the gallery space loosened the I of Karyn as author, for a we laboring and navigating scales of labor and duration. This is in keeping with a thought put forward by artist Paul Ramírez Jonas in conversation with Olivier while discussing her public project *Inbound: Houston*:

> I imagine that since most permanent monuments require
> more than one maker the perception of individual
> authorship is diluted; but I like to think that because
> a monument almost always pre-supposes a collective
> story or image, then authorship does not stick to it
> in quite the same way that it does to a sculpture.[7]

Consider *Fortified*. The monumental work required many hands to install. Five people were dedicated to building this wall and four more offered rolling support of the vibrant cacophonous play of color between brick and repurposed clothing, speaking to painting and formal concern. The crux of the chromatic polyphony of clothing as mortar results not from one mind or plan, but rather the variations and densities reflect the distinct decisions and proclivities of individual workers. It's all quite ad hoc: with no clear rule for how to

---

7   *Inbound: Houston*, 42.

use clothing as mortar between bricks, each must wedge their way. Each formal author-laborer set, leveled, and locked idiosyncratically with every other author-laborer into this expanse of brick and clothing. The can-do author of *Fortified*, to a degree, is the duration of labors, architecture's version of manual authorial agency: did you do a careful job?

Finished, the wall is a collective story: wailing wall, border wall, sheltering wall, back against the wall. *Fortified* does what walls do—divide, block, direct, impose—as it visually engages and seduces. Despite recognition of the humorous and divergent collar, waistband, sleeve, sock, bra, and shirttail bits tucked, peeking between the bricks, the full avalanche of clothing as you round the wall to the back stuns. The weight of thousands of bricks is materially understood; the weight of hundreds of used garments is emotionally felt. And as with any misguided wall aimed at immigration, *Fortified* speaks to an absence exponentially larger than its presence. The clothing does not accumulate as a gorgeous stand-in for bodies or work as metaphor. Each item was worn by someone not present in the space and traces a real path of repurposed transition in taste, size, location, economic level, or life. It is a literal accumulation of absence. The dazzling formal brilliance of color, line, plane, tone, geometry, and disorder is a precariously political beauty formed through painterly flourish via material change and collective effort.

Wedged clothing has no structural strength to permanently set brick. It is make-do and one recognizes brick stacked and balanced and held tentatively after brick stacked and balanced and held tentatively absent the firm setting of concrete. With the tug of a thread or a dozen this precarious structure is undone in the same hand-by-hand manner it can be built. Brick unstacked and unbalanced after brick. I revisited *Fortified*, alone, after all business as usual ended in spring 2020. This solitary pause was no silence: navigating the short four-step shift from flat front brick wall to the backside cloth mass of *Fortified* loudly pushes out enough rational engagements threaded through with the strength of repurposed clothing, the precarity of the bricks, the abstracted record of absent bodies and labor hours to divert. Speculative torrents rush in, such as those offered by poet Alexis Pauline Gumbs, "so when everything imploded it was not the breaking bones and the lost flesh that shocked them. everyone knows the human body is fragile. what shocked them was how fast a wall could fall."[8]

The reason I was in the closed gallery alone at all was because the body is indeed fragile. We know this. Walls pretend otherwise. And yet we know any wall, no matter how imposing, can be taken down. What is remarkable with *Fortified* is Olivier's desire to build a wall that is a fragile, fleeting soft mass of scattering pleasures and a wobbly structure that beautifully overwhelms the rigid, geometric solidly intransigent rule of massed brick from its start.

Seemingly similar in formal logic to *Fortified*, the shoes shoved and shored in place by fitted fabric seams in *Car Cover and Export Shoes* have none of the cascading, undulating flow and delighting disjunction in front to back. This disjunction is in huddled unity as a decidedly dank heap of degraded footwear camouflaged as car. The material difference between old clothes and used shoes in noticeable smell, greased touch, and degraded rubber residue which leaves dirty oily tracks on any surface it touches, sets a qualitative shift in perception of value. And therefore, potential for an invitation to beauty. Different too is the intended path of this material tonnage. The used clothing is sourced from suppliers that gather garments for resale and thrift; the shoes sourced from suppliers that gather footwear for shipment to other countries in charity, as disaster relief, or simple down-market recirculation. Both *Fortified* and *Car Cover and Export Shoes* coagulate the movement of capital value, abstracting political routes of collective impediment (wall), the promise of individualized luxury (car), repurposed value (clothing), and castoff dole (shoes), along accumulated potential or disdain. But only one becomes an Audi.

----

8   Alexis Pauline Gumbs, *M Archive* (Durham: Duke University Press, 2018), 144.

What these monuments of movement share is an irreverence in gesture and an absurdity of construction: clothing for mortar, precarious prop as vehicle. Olivier's materials multiply in overwhelming gestural quantities never larger than life. They require personal labor to assemble a whole from industrially fabricated components. Each is made at human scale. The resulting structures are at once remarkably direct (wall, car) and infinitely variable: a precarious, dazzlingly colorful bygone wall of no solid place, a German luxury import car formed of worthless shoes for export, likely to somewhere in the global south. And the materials come at a cost. These costs are relatively straightforward: bundles of shoes or clothes for a dollar a pound, the price of an Audi. The costs are also accumulative: requiring the labor of five people over seven days to make a wall thirty feet long and fifteen feet tall. Some costs too are harder to record in a ledger: displacement, imbalance of power, withdrawal of resources. All of this sets some spaces to be resource rich in their accumulation of potential while designing others to labor purposefully with resource poverty, and as Fanny Howe describes in her book *Night Philosophy*:

> Poverty, writes Leonardo Boff, "is a way of being by
> which the individual lets things be what they are; one
> refuses to dominate them, subjugate them, and make
> them the objects of the will to power." The importance
> of this definition to a political artist in this century
> lies in its moral imperative. While you are enjoined
> to combat the outrage of poverty, you are also guided
> toward the values of a possessionless underclass.[9]

Let's revisit Olivier's commentary on *The Battle Is Joined*:

> Maybe monuments can be instruments that offer us a
> mirror to give witness to ourselves, our community,
> our city, or to the world. Or maybe they implore us to be

---

9   Fanny Howe, "Franciscan," in *Night Philosophy* (Brussels: Divided Publishing, 2020), 79.

<blockquote>aware of the present moment and allow us to reflect on our shared complicated histories. It can be a space that interrogates our histories and poses questions about our past that can speak about its impact today.[10]</blockquote>

My intent in sharing excerpts from the writings of the artist and others is to find a parallel to Olivier's manner of posing questions that speak to the impacts of a complicated past, to reflect her use of preexisting forms to recalibrate definition: "And now that I think I know this table, how can I change it?" That the monuments of *Fortified* and *Car Cover and Export Shoes* are made of the repurposed carries with this fact nouns and verbs as guarantees that the visual form will not land a singular narrative destination. Connections pluralize in the background as easily as we differentiate a drooping sweater from a worn-out sneaker. The figure-ground relationship can thread ideas and sentences, as well as material categories to catch refractions and re-see economic through-lines, socialized patterning, absent historical presences and what? As Olivier has noted, "There's this assumption that monuments are built because we've collectively decided something's important to celebrate, honor, to cherish. But we know that we don't have equal voices in that mandate."[11] So how can we listen with uneven partitions? Olivier's efforts via form and denotation show how people and monuments often reward history, retell valor, honor loss, become displaced, and expire without collective agreement on their costs or consensus on values, often, in part, by refusing proper nouns and recognizable histories of traditional monument men. Valuative words do not settle easily these architectures of power, a continual negotiation she herself stresses as a crucial emotional power and reflective political weight as a sculptor. "And now that I think I know this table, how can I change it?"

---

10   "Monumental Exchange 2," 266.

11   Ibid, 265.

The oldest work in the exhibition, *It's Not Over 'Til It's Over* (2004), offers solitary pleasure on a starkly public stage. It is a carousel after all, with the entertaining smile proffered by such basic joys. There are playful colors and a string of lights, sans the usual menagerie or even chariots—just an old-fashioned school desk chair. There is no calliope music, only the sound of mechanical rotation and material wear. The ride's constant clockwise motion, rather than the more usual counterclockwise stop and start, feels glacial at five minutes per rotation. Still, your trip is also quite generous: how often do you have five minutes to yourself in public? It is calming to sit alone for a full rotation, with forlorn time to awkwardly settle in and just think. "Time is merciful, but that does not mean it is not heartbreaking."[12] Time is measured in ruthlessly standardized increments for public synchronicity rather than private revelry, work days of wage hours, of your time left. Phenomenologically the clockwise turn of Olivier's carousel re-emphasizes the rotation of the standard digital clock of capital rather than a carousel's usual playful analog gallop against the tide of everyday chore. We—our desires—are never fully synchronized in public. There may be a million ways to personally navigate public space, but this stream has a steady current, and this is where public space often begins to feel paced by others. In fact, public space often presses most unjustly upon private identities and desires when these individualized rhythms step into public view. The generosity of *It's Not Over 'Til It's Over* turns bittersweet as a place to private in public orbit, a little slower alongside. Seated, you might just get a sense that it is never over until it's over, if ever.

As a monument or memorial, in the gallery *It's Not Over 'Til It's Over* is nearly hermetic compared to the other works. The protective canopy darkens the gray platform from the overhead even white of gallery lighting. And where do you look? There are excruciatingly long seconds with nothing ahead besides bare wall. Making eye contact with others, usually a fleeting pulse-quickening affair, has an

---

12   Anne Boyer, "This Imaginary Half-Nothing, Time," in *A Handbook of Disappointed Fate* (Brooklyn: Ugly Duckling Presse, 2018), 199.

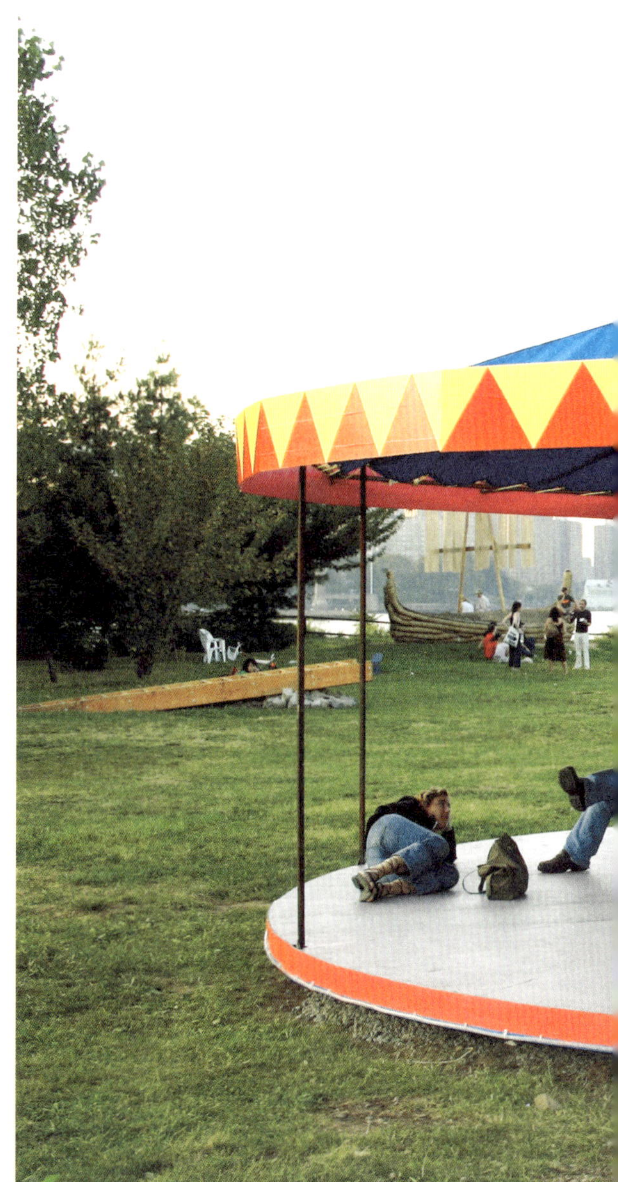

It's Not Over 'Til It's Over, 2004
Steel, wood, fabric, rope lighting,
rotating floor, and chair
14 × 24 ft. diameter
Courtesy of the artist and
Tanya Bonakdar Gallery, New York / Los Angeles

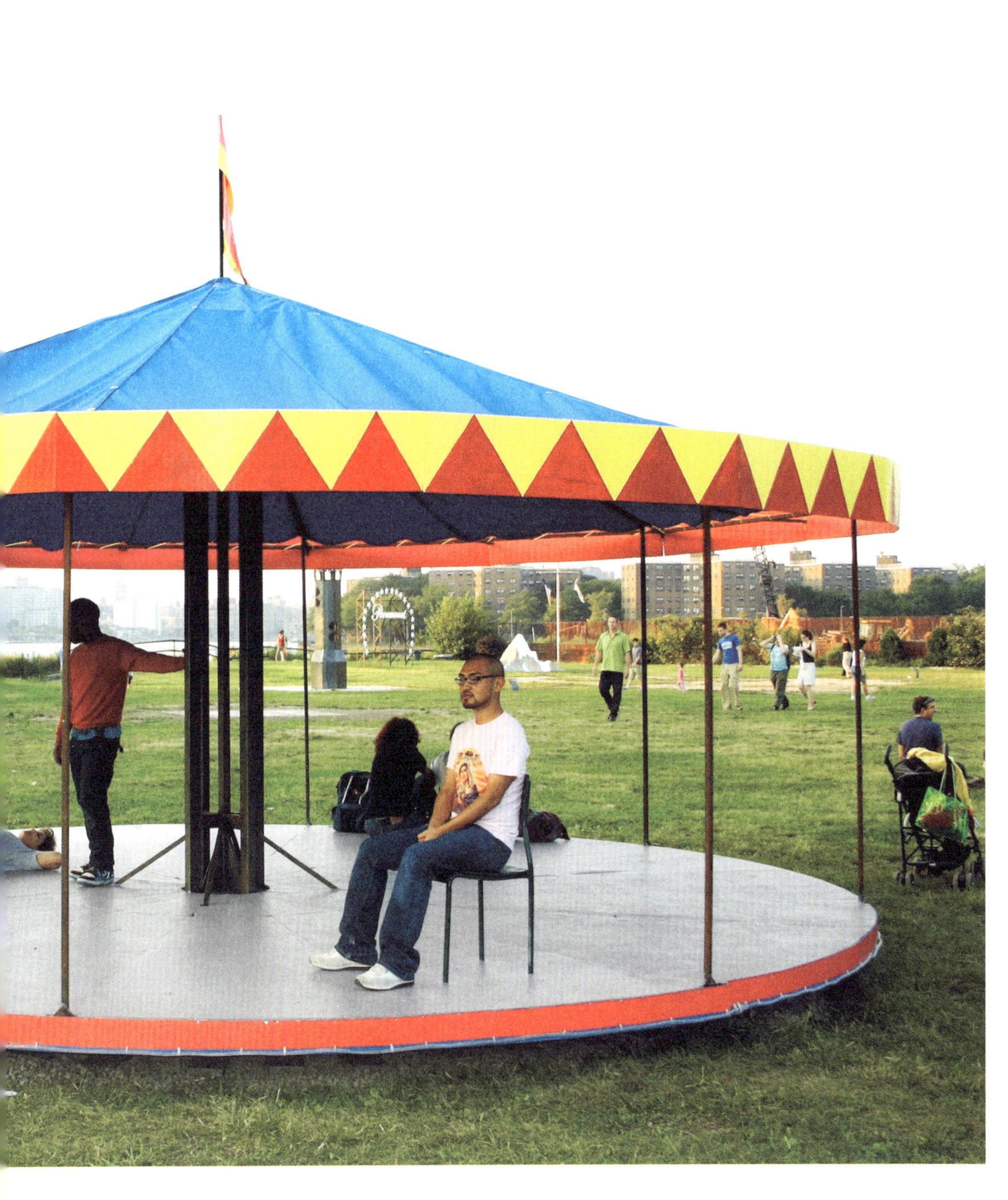

absurdly glacial drag that accumulates in mechanistic discomfort. You haven't yet moved past. You are secluded from others, even those who may be standing on the carousel nearby. You have the seat, still. The rest of the exhibition is pushed farther away as if in another brighter, more lively space while you simultaneously hold your privileged navigating pivot along this joyful slow-turning view. You become, in effect, the steady centerpiece of collective rotation through which the exhibition turns: from here, of central importance is just how you are who.

> The domestic sphere, that urgent foundation for natality,
> will here be considered in terms of a mediating skin,
> rather than in terms of a private interiority conceptually
> opposed to a social outside. This mediating condition will be
> inflected temporally, rather than spatially, since its limit is
> less structurally architectural than flexibly transformative:
> the taking in and preparation of food, of erotic encounter,
> of various modes of work, of reproductive labor, of the
> production of an affective surplus and the constant re-
> initiation into freshened verbal motility—the *domus* is the
> place of rhythmic protection of the vulnerable body, while
> sleeping, in illness, age, and childhood, often while eating
> and washing, while resting, while talking and working.
> So the domestic sphere isn't private just as the body and
> its modes of conviviality, reproduction and care aren't
> private—it expresses a complex temporality that includes
> coded information from the past as it moves always in
> the light of the polyvalent and self-inventing present. In
> terms of subjectivity and temporality, the domestic sphere
> emerges as an embodied vector that breaks open, floods
> the habitual containment of the public-private binary.[13]

13 Robertson, *Thresholds*, 4.

If we require evidence for this assertion by Robertson (we really do not), the raw exposures of 2020 in public health and social civility underscore all evidence in terrors of accumulated cases. Fragile and constantly under threat, those at the outskirts of citizenship account for a sweepingly large segment of the US population and pedantic political vitriol. The domestic is under continual public judgment. These factors are an important private landscape to publicly feel when seated on *It's Not Over 'Til It's Over*. And they are felt in the simple act of rotating alone in public. The mind just has to wander, as there isn't *that* much to take in from the surrounding gallery, and no horizon. The astringent clockwise charms no doubt reflective of palpable pangs along Robertson's *mediating skin* and *embodied vectors* bared. This peripheral shifting with time is not unpleasant; it is the drag of conviviality, reproduction, and care, perceptually compounded, humored evidence that we shall see what we *shall* see. The chair makes a wonderfully covered and awkwardly exposed vehicle for a bewilderingly drawn-out joyride as a public-private being.

> no one invented time. it's just that the sun and moon did
> what they did and we felt it. so no one had to abolish time
> either. it was just that we couldn't see the sky anymore and
> we didn't feel ourselves breathing. so whenever it was,
> we had no choice but to be present. some people believed
> that time was moving backward, which would have been
> nice, if it meant we could undo what we had done.[14]

Turning to the three more recent sculptures, these reflect Olivier's 2018–2019 year of study in Rome, where she investigated the city's collateral accumulation of ruins, histories, and public dissembling, and, more importantly, how these impact the present. The sculptures offer a chance to attune ourselves to her care for minute and minor gestures that accumulate via logic rather than materials to trace large, often-overlooked patterns. These works also reflect the coagulation of progressing time and the perpetual irresolution inherent in the structure of cities, as decades of boundaries and fortifications and burials leave traces as infrastructure for later resettlements and redefinitions of publics.

Begun at the artist's studio at the American Academy in Rome and finished in ICA's first-floor gallery in January 2020, *Moving the Obelisk* restages the well-worn historical patterns of capture and transport. Originating in Egypt, an obelisk traditionally is a four-sided tapered monolith. Pharaohs often repurposed the obelisks of previous dynasties for their own temples. Then, beginning 30 BCE, Romans regularly ransacked Egyptian temples, looting these treasures in particular and presenting them as territorial gifts to such an extent that today there are more than twice as many standing obelisks outside of Egypt as within. *Moving the Obelisk* replays this trajectory of displacement and traffic. "It speaks of the absurdity of what it would mean to make these sixty-foot-tall, thirty-ton obelisks. And what does it mean for me to make my own monument when we are at a time in this country thinking about monuments?"[15] Olivier and a crew dismantled not a stone monolith but a cartoonish simulation made of local dirt and discarded cardboard boxes held together by tape and wood in four-tiered balance—a janky makeshift private monument constructed in her Rome studio. The team packed the components and documented their transit and restaging in Philadelphia.

With this gesture, Olivier diminishes the awe and stature accorded to a solid mass of stone to focus on the actions that historically surround these forms: conquering, dismantling, transporting, disfiguring, resetting. The video documentation of transport challenges the obelisk's stable verticality. So much of the history of these monuments is about out-of-balance economies, trade, and power for which they become mere temporary vessels. Watching the packing, carting, sawing, turning, repairing, and hoisting, it is the

---

15   Katy Donoghue, "Karyn Olivier: Thinking about monuments, memory, and absence," *Whitewall Magazine*, Summer 2020, 63.

broad lateral moments spanning geographies that activate Olivier's obelisk. The resting verticality at journey's end reads almost as afterthought for this seductively surfaced structure.[16] The meaning is all in movement. Through such displacements of monumentality, Olivier's obelisk reminds us (as might a casual walk in Rome) that civic space accrues through the weight of peoples' labor, and that citizenship is too often built with a negative space that denies such labor—noticeable only if we pause and return to looking with special attention for outstanding debts traded and staged.

"Could there be "revenant" events like one talks about "revenant" souls?"[17] Alas, yes. With the most recent work in this exhibition, *May 12, 1985*, Olivier asked each visitor to carry one carnation; the flowers were handed out at ICA's front desk instead of the usual metal admission tabs. This gesture has roots in Philadelphia rather than Rome, though it builds on a similar recognition of how unresolved histories get embedded in the seemingly stable structures of a city. MOVE was a Black liberation group officially founded in 1972 and based in West Philadelphia. Their anarcho-primitivist lifestyle and political activities under the overarching mission—to protect life— brought periodic confrontations with authorities. The most heated exchange, following local police serving an eviction notice and arrest warrants, ended in mass tragedy, as the ensuing stand-off concluded with authorities ordering a police helicopter to drop a bomb on the MOVE compound. The fire killed eleven group members, including five children, and engulfed the neighborhood, destroying approximately sixty-five homes on and near the 6200 block of Osage Avenue on Monday, May 13, 1985.

When it comes to communal organizations, the government time and again displays an ignorance in how to address and conduct

---

16   In this, *Moving the Obelisk* parallels *The Battle Is Joined* to erase any thought that a monument becomes a monument in staid verticality. See "Monumental Exchange 2," 265: "We're just so used to that verticality of looking up, reverence equals looking up at this imposing structure, but maybe now one is asked to look around and this object becomes a living, breathing entity."

17   Raul Ruiz, *The Wit of the Staircase* (Paris: Dis Voir, 2012), 58.

negotiations, especially when the collective is not white. At the heart of the problem is an inability to understand the difference in structure between self-reliance and organized authority in communal-minded people:

> Instead of imagining personal rights in continual conflict with social order, communitarian philosophies understand the individual as both the creator and the product in community. Communitarianism doesn't deny the value of autonomy, but shifts the focus of political or public decision-making to the community as foundation for meaning and authority.[18]

The state's misunderstanding never fails to ignite tragedies large and small. As novelist Hari Kunzru succinctly and brutally summed up the US government's time-honored carceral disdain and racialized blunt force: "When you are powerless, your belief or disbelief is irrelevant. No one gives a damn about what you believe. But if some reality believes in you, then you must live it. You can't say no thank you. You can't say I don't want this. If horror believes in you, there's nothing to be done."[19] The horrific belief of Philadelphia police cared nothing for the communal decision-making of MOVE. The reality of policed structural racism and class warfare didn't see public agrarian dreams of self-determination, didn't see the care and focus on reproducibility; they saw only the horrible affront they interpreted in MOVE's disregard for the sanctity of individuated ownership. Death for the state was more justified and real than doubt of private property. The state sided with tragedy rather than joy.

Only on rare prismatic occasions does communal thinking along tenderly sensitive threads overcome the uninquisitive overaction of violent state structures. One such case took place eighty years before the crime perpetrated against MOVE. Anna Jarvis (1864–1948),

---

18 Judy D. Whipps, "Jane Addam's Social Thought as a Model for a Pragmatist-Feminist Communitarianism," *Hypatia*, 19, No. 2, *Women in the American Philosophical Tradition 1800–1930* (Spring, 2004), 119.

19 Hari Kunzru, *White Tears* (New York: Alfred A. Knopf, 2017), 227.

a West Virginia native who moved to Philadelphia, worked tirelessly to establish a day of honor, as she told the *Philadelphia Inquirer* in May 1913,

> to make men and women realize their individual responsibility
> to right the wrongs of motherhood and childhood, not
> only in the home but also in the industrial world, and in
> the name of 'mother' to inspire men to carry forward the
> work for the home, which would mean not only its uplift,
> but would deepen their brotherhood toward each other.[20]

This inflection of the domestic motherhood into industralized process is a remarkably prescient recognition of the mediated skin and embodied vectors of the domestic Robertson mapped nearly a century later. Jarvis began her campaign for a national Mother's Day in 1905, and the day was first celebrated in West Virginia in 1908. The carnation, the favorite flower of Jarvis's mother, became the emblem of the holiday: red if your mother was alive, white if she were dead. By 1911 every state had recognized the holiday, even as the idea was still roundly mocked by Congress. So in 1914 a presidential proclamation declared the second Sunday in May as Mother's Day. It was on the second Sunday in May 1985 that police served warrants to MOVE.

Olivier's work makes space to lovingly acknowledge unresolved and overlapping facets of histories as embedded in our cities and spaces and, most importantly, carried within each of us as an individual and a citizen. With *May 12, 1985*, by returning to the Sunday of celebration prior to tragedy, Olivier's carnations stage something akin to Robertson's "complex temporality that includes coded information from the past as it moves always in the light of the polyvalent and self-inventing present." Her carnations, in their simple direct accumulation of mass via material dispersal, one by one gain heft along

---

20 Patricia Madej, "Why do we celebrate Mother's Day? Thank this Philadelphia woman,," *The Philadelphia Inquirer*, May 12, 2019, https://www.inquirer.com/news/mothers-day-philadelphia-anna-jarvis-history-20190512.html

invisible complex temporalities that are more delineating as borders than those of country or state: have/have not, new/repurposed, gathered/individuated, passed/passed-on, welcomed/unwelcomed. Along these lines, lives (present and absent) and memories (acknowledged and hidden) cross and touch—sometimes in harmonious unison, but more often with friction and compound pressure. Like the delicate, warming beauty of navigating your city with an unexpectedly received red carnation in hand, the attendant fragrant smiles and memorials and histories against the erasure of silent concrete years underfoot abound in each floral red beacon.

Installation photography cannot capture the full experience of Olivier's *Summoned*, her second audio work. Every twenty-two minutes, a thirty-second recording of the noon bells from San Giovanni Crisostomo in Giuliano di Lecce, Italy, chimes dispersed through four speakers. The experience is fairly common to anyone who has navigated a religious city or town through sound, suddenly enveloped in an echoing call to pause, to worship, or to simply register the changing hour—if, that is, you hear the call. Summons to civic attentiveness today are more likely to be served by paper or push notifications to networked individuals than broadcast for a populace in crosscurrent traffics. A quaint analog chiming of our civic spaces increasingly threatened by digital precision, all squares and open space are bartered, sold, and traded for naming, transforming spaces for anyone to spaces of specific someones who exert excess influence on what is public and for how long.

The church in Giuliano di Lecce is dedicated to St. John Chrysostom, regarded for his golden tone and passionate sermons. Setting her periodic rejoinder off standard clock interval allows for surprise of return and slight shift of the day's clock. You feel an inability to mark the standardized regimental measure in this summons. The multifocal clanging and fade of distant bells cycles in and out of sync with standard hours for a jubilant interruption of counterregister. Of what?

Given this spectral shimmering, the great fear is that vernaculars could disappear, quantified then subsumed by the instrumental grammar of capital. The fragility of speech, whose proper location is anywhere people face and receive and act towards and for one another, could be anywhere, as we have discerned, and yet it seems that there are fewer anywheres, and many somewheres, fewer anybodies, and many somebodies. The public sphere and the private sphere, those attractive products of Romanticism and Enlightenment economic thought, each radiate a mystique. Even the political functions as nostalgia and not event. In the current economy, public and private lose their differentiation, but not in a manner convivial to freedom.[21]

The trick is to perceive the nostalgias in material memory to reinscribe the differentiations of the public-private binary and expose complicities. Olivier's multivocal chiming return is a reminder that for any meaningful conversation about shared values, atonement, wrongdoing, or healing to occur (qualities conducive to growing freedoms), our monuments and memorials must be erected not as unwavering permanent markers of triumphs and tragedies, but as asynchronous markers of compound temporalities. Alongside an array of domestics. When the MOVE compound was attacked, I wasn't of voting age and I lived 640 miles away. In that I may not be guilty of the city government's atrocity, but in moving to Philadelphia twenty-five years later I signed on in some respect to complicity with the local government that still cannot even define the bombing as an act deserving of apology, let alone as a crime.[22] I settled in place along an embodied vector with a politics. Within this complicity is

21   Robertson, *Thresholds*, 13.

22   The city of Philadelphia did eventually release a milquetoast formal apology and little else on November 12, 2020.

power for memory or erasure and movement or stasis and acquiescence or dissension. Though these *or*'s are probably more accurately pronounced as *and*'s.

We—complicity's monuments—are routinely amidst revenants if we tend to our settings. We are complicit connections for ambient emotion and navigate unacknowledged politics as domestic monuments to the politics of spectral shimmering. For those who fear that dismantling Confederate monuments means dismantling history, fret not—this past hasn't yet passed on. *Everything That's Alive Moves*, the exhibition title, was borrowed from a talking point used in interviews by MOVE's John Africa as a way to explain the group's name. I read in the phrase a clarifying and useful definition: *if* something is alive, it *moves*, be it a crow, a dogwood, a morel, or a sea cucumber, even currency. If Confederate monuments are now on the move it is evidence that they and the white supremacist systems they represent remain alive. This racist spirit still too often defines what is permanent—in stone, marble, and bronze—in the United States. This lost cause pandemic is more stubbornly rooted, infectious, and crippling to economic and social health than any biological virus.

These considerations are not backscattering projections or metaphoric refraction. On Sunday, June 28, 2020, "My Body Is a Confederate Monument," an opinion piece by Caroline Randall Williams, was published in the *New York Times*. An astute declaration of a body's deeply ingrained knotted powers and histories, the column would rip open a view to the personal weight of our social fabric:

> If there are those who want to remember the legacy
> of the Confederacy, if they want monuments,
> well, then, my body is a monument.
>
> Dead Confederates are honored all over this country—with
> cartoonish private statues, solemn public monuments and
> even in the names of United States Army bases. It fortifies
> and heartens me to witness the protests against this

practice and the growing clamor from serious, nonpartisan public servants to redress it. But there are still those—like President Trump and the Senate majority leader, Mitch McConnell—who cannot understand the difference between rewriting and reframing the past. I say it is not a matter of "airbrushing" history, but of adding a new perspective.

I am a Black, Southern woman, and of my immediate
white male ancestors, all of them were rapists. My
very existence is a relic of slavery and Jim Crow.[23]

Back in 1985, Indiana's "Debby with Monument" swept aside shallow and sanctimonious aesthetic squabbles in the *Titled Arc* debacle to identify how Serra's abstract sculpture's space was drawn with little regard for the—to them—unimportant people whose real existence was even more of an abstract projection than the COR-TEN steel curve for sculptor and commissioning force. For these overlooked individuals, however, there was no abstraction, or rather, they were desperately trying to protect the abstraction of citizenship from the real horrors perpetrated by the state's belief. That public plaza was a real space of traffic toward or against pain and contestation under daily negotiation. These mutable facts never receive their permanent contracts or timeless honors. They know only questions and tides. Williams too records lies that fly in stone-faced formation as ever-present dogs and fleas clouding our views of real space:

The dream version of the Old South never existed. Any
manufactured monument to that time in that place tells
half a truth at best. The ideas and ideals it purports to
honor are not real. To those who have embraced these
delusions: now is the time to re-examine your position.

23   Caroline Randall Williams, "My Body Is a Confederate Monument," *New York Times Sunday Review*, June 28, 2020, 4.

Either you have been blind to a truth that my body's
story forces you to see or you really do mean to honor the
oppressors at the expense of the oppressed, and you must
at last acknowledge your investment in a legacy of hate.

Either way, I say the monuments of stone and metal,
the monuments of cloth and wood, all the man-made
monuments, must come down. I defy any sentimental
Southerner to defend our ancestors to me. I am quite literally
made of the reasons to strip them of their laurels.[24]

Not every unseen thread is an abstraction and complicit never implies consent or commensurability or conviviality.

We move everyday with the clear understanding that the sunshine on our skin—now, as we go about the day—is eight minutes old owing to distance and physical limitations of the speed of light. We move energized and enlivened by this light. Yet we understand how excess time spent in this energizing eight-minute-old light damages skin and weathers every structure. So why bristle at the idea that we too are powered by and exposed to old, potentially damaging energy when we contemplate a wall, ride a carousel, move an obelisk, offer a flower, heed a call, and live in a country where pernicious powers defend oppressive monuments. The bricks, steel, bronze, cardboard, and dirt of our landscape are not harboring inert passed histories. We need inviting ways of looking and listening to the past that allow for reverberation along compound temporalities that mark the now and chime the arrival of asynchronous what's yets. As long as there is a temporal connection with histories—to people, to places, to emotions, to politics, to stories—there remain fertile grammars which carnival-esque patterns may bloom and cherished individuals carry out.

Olivier's work offers just such tense settings for beautiful questions in a gorgeous living in spite of and in recognition of hardship. *Traffic Barricade With Fruit* (2011) provides a clear and sly

---

24   Randall Williams, 4.

reminder of this. For two months, this sculpture stood innocuously on a Mexico City sidewalk. The standard concrete traffic barricade was not an obstruction or a barrier to movement, instead served as a countertop or display shelf. Every day fresh fruit was presented and replenished and every day these fruits were taken. The sculpture distantly recalled the roadside fruit sellers encountered along many heavily trafficked roadways the world over. When such barricades appear along the medians, vendors have no problem using them as makeshift sales tables. Olivier modeled this repurposing of material understanding if not the transactional economy. Hers were decidedly small offerings: single pieces of fruit. The gentle gesture neither disregarded the hardships experienced by passersby nor rewarded valor; each fruit simply paused usual rhythmic expectations of civic life long enough to offer something in addition. Some days we struggle. Some days we breeze by. Some days the barricades are against us. Other days these barricades are offerings. Some days level off. Others end in excesses. Some days I'd prefer to see you pausing with a delicious apple alongside the things that used to be and those that still are, slowing just enough to appreciate the edges refracted with every bite.

> The present tense is the tense of emergency and
> ego. I don't like it telling a story. The past is the most
> convincing and carries a shadow on its back like a bag of
> stones. The past is always a little melancholy. Slate gray,
> sunless. The past is the best tense for storytelling. The
> storyteller drops the bag and sits down to look it over.

> That there is a future tense is astounding. A night-thought
> soon to be abolished by daylight. See through it like water.[25]

---

25   Howe, "Tense and Raving," *Night Philosophy,* 92.

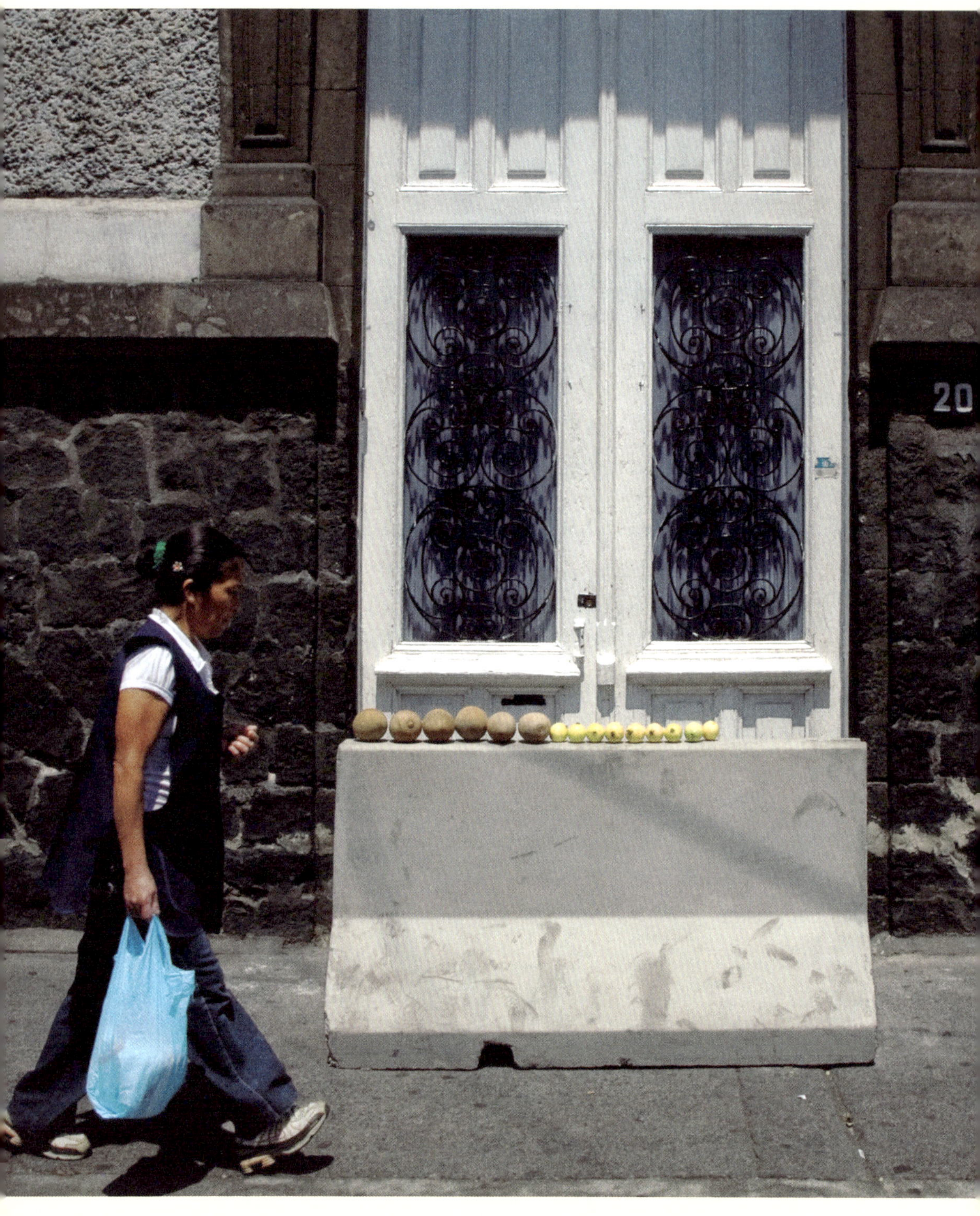

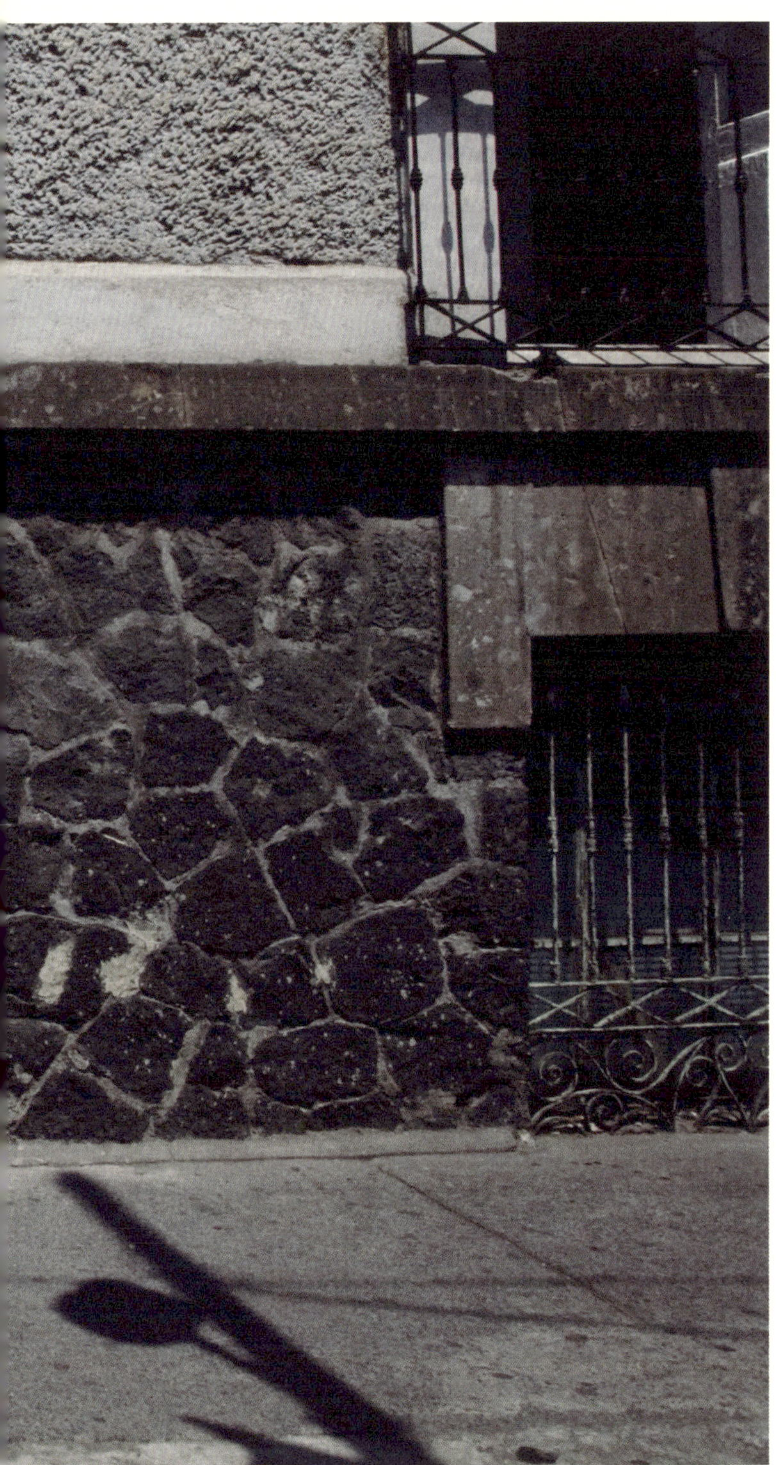

Traffic Barricade With Fruit, 2011
Mexico City, Mexico
57 × 31 × 22 in.
Courtesy of the artist

Installation Views

ICA
UB ART GALLERIES

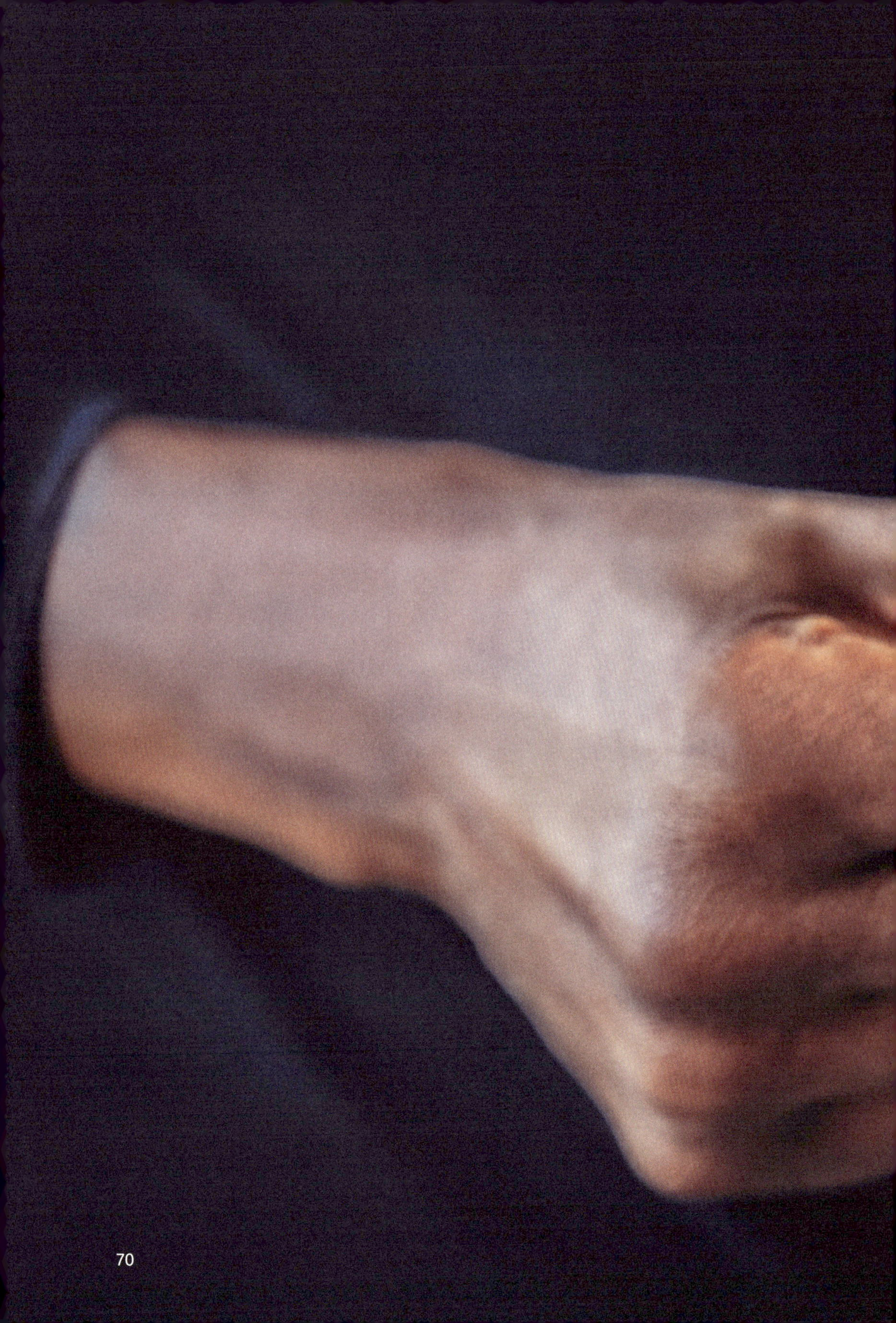

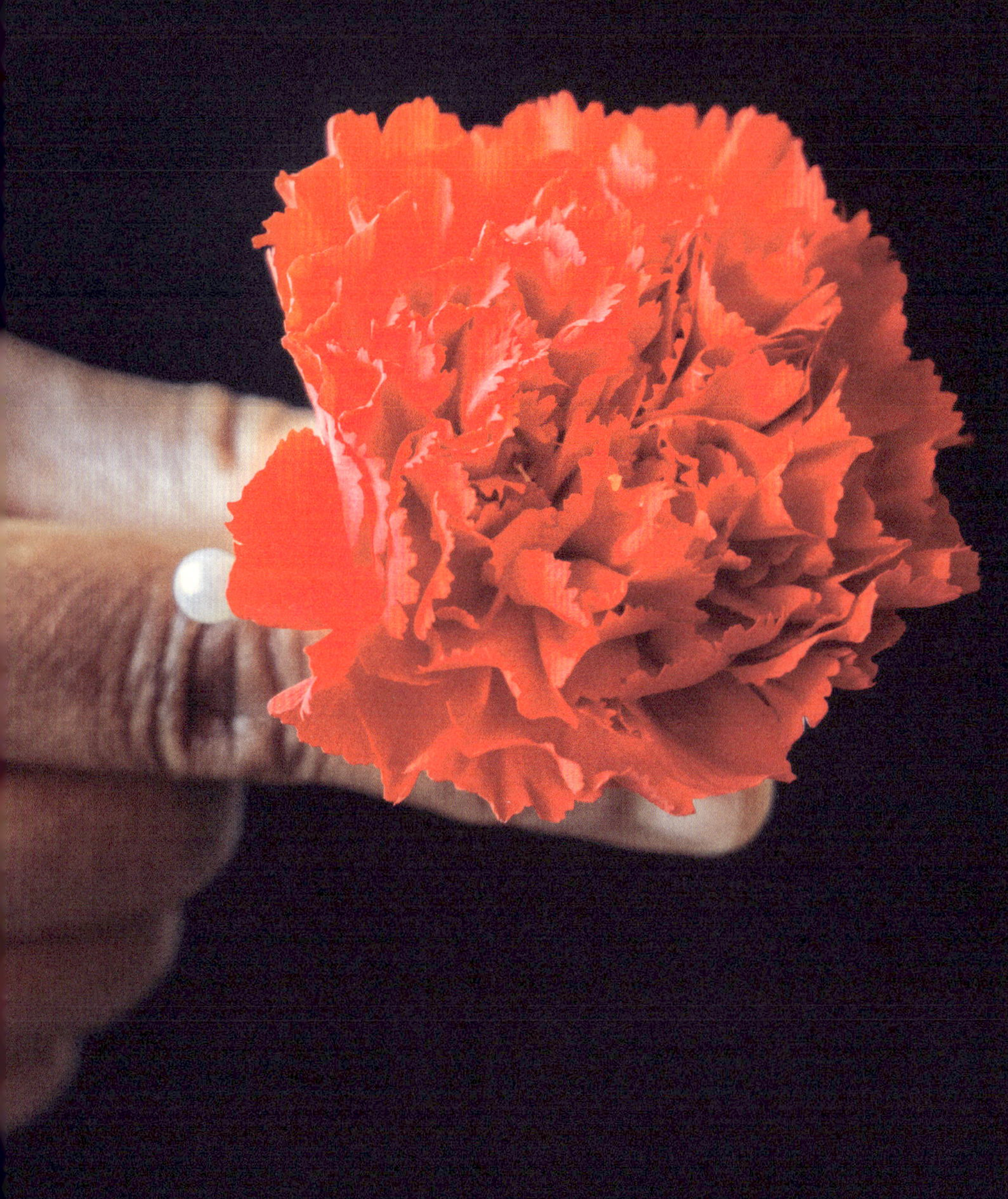

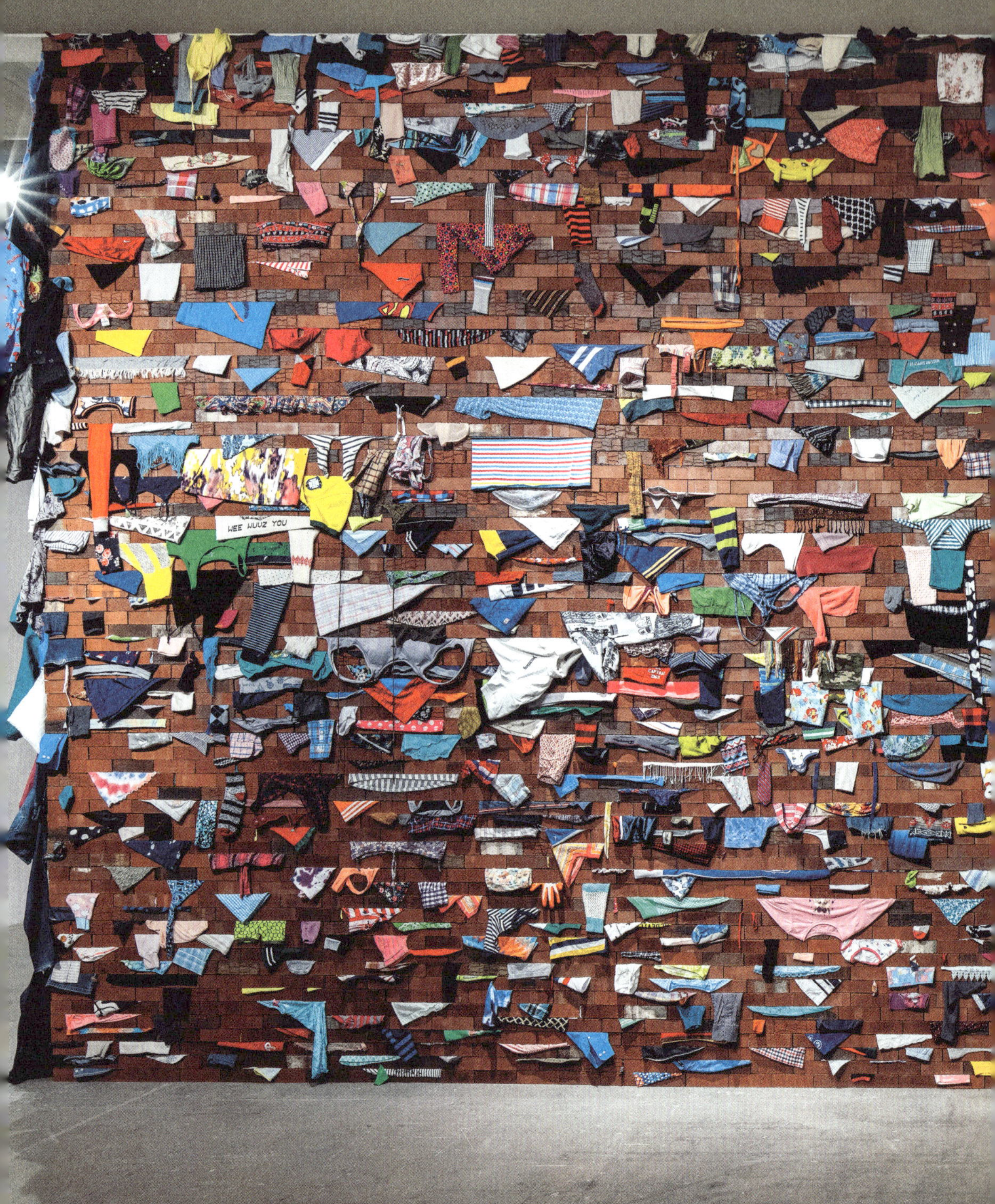
WEE WUUZ YOU

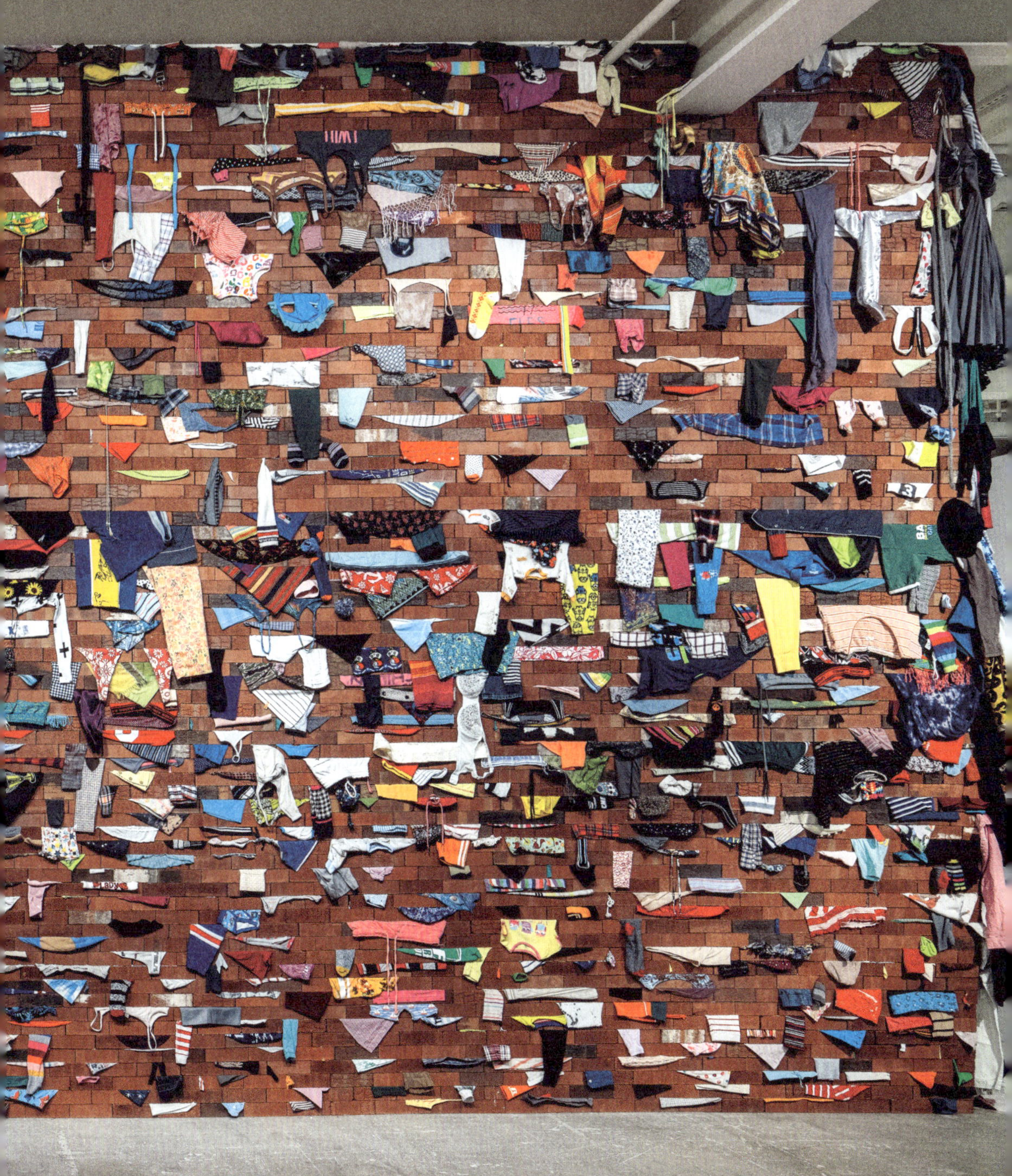

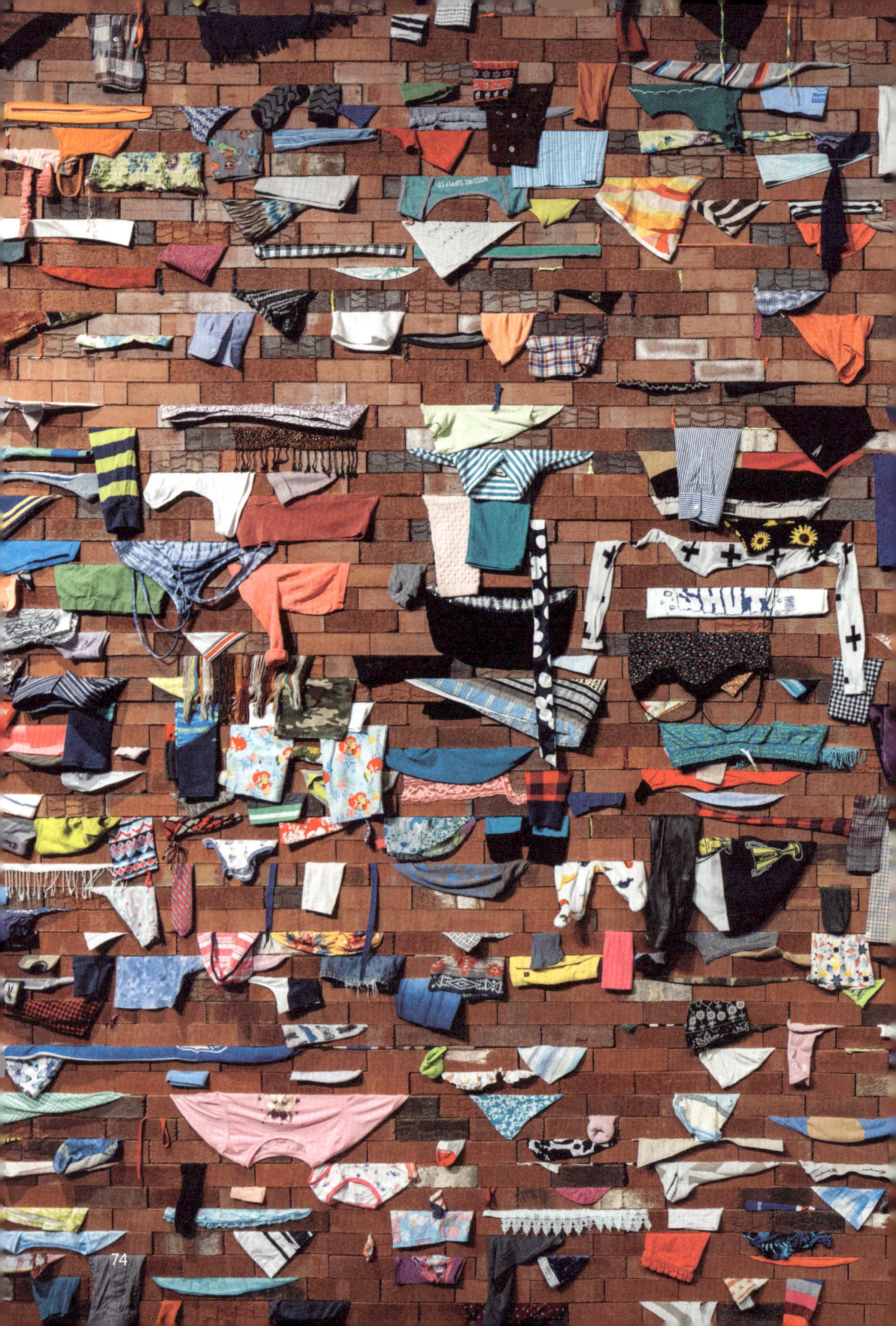

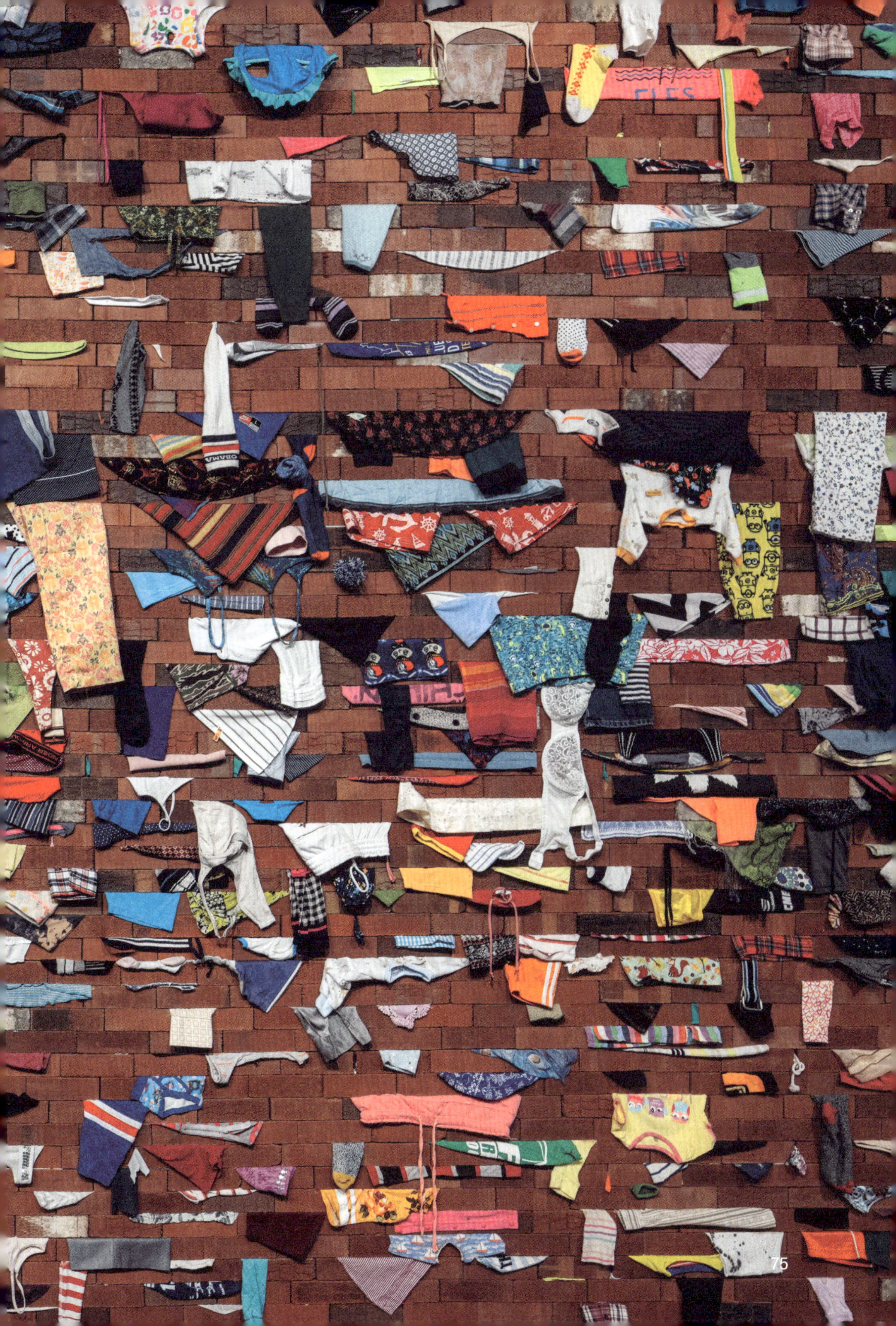

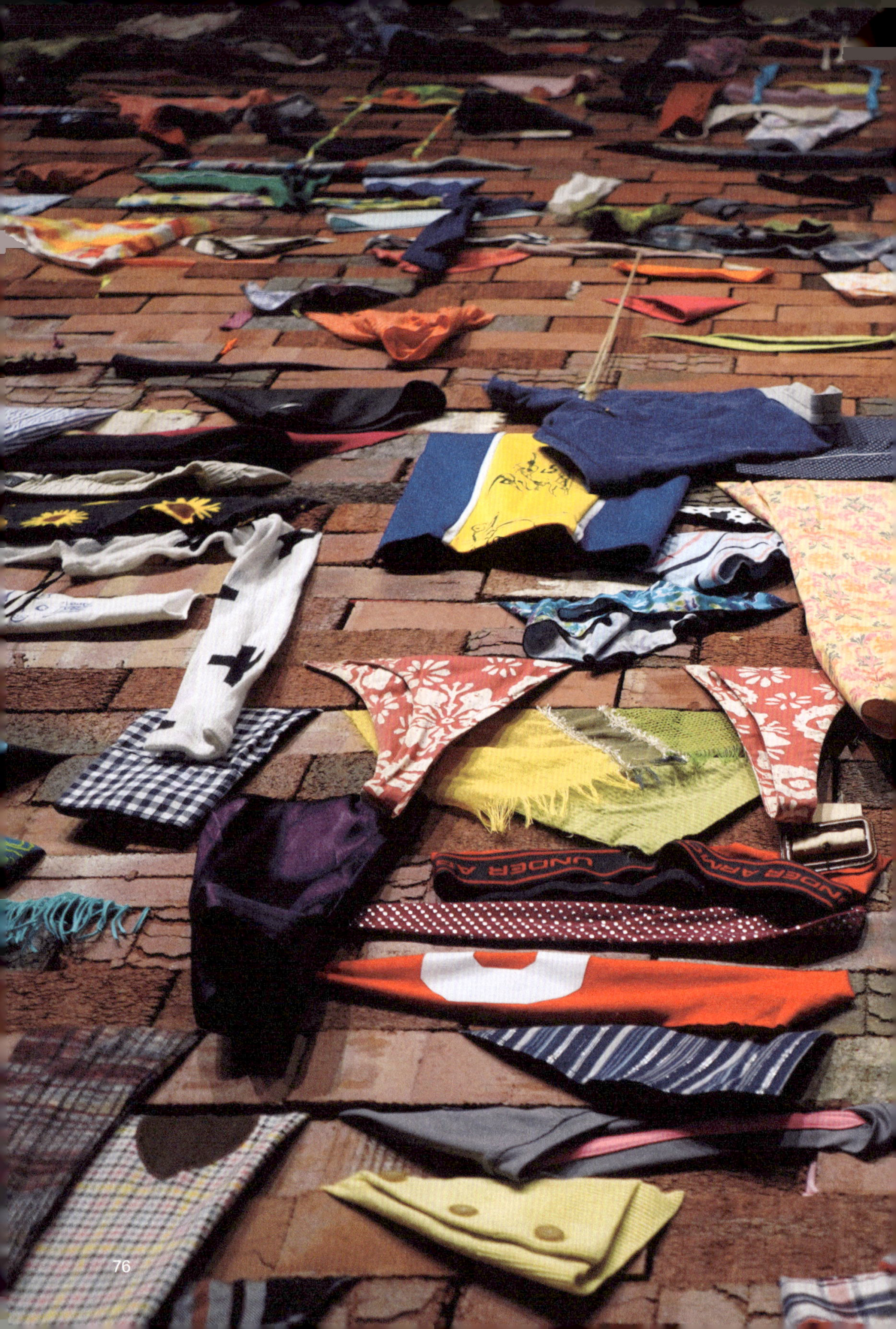

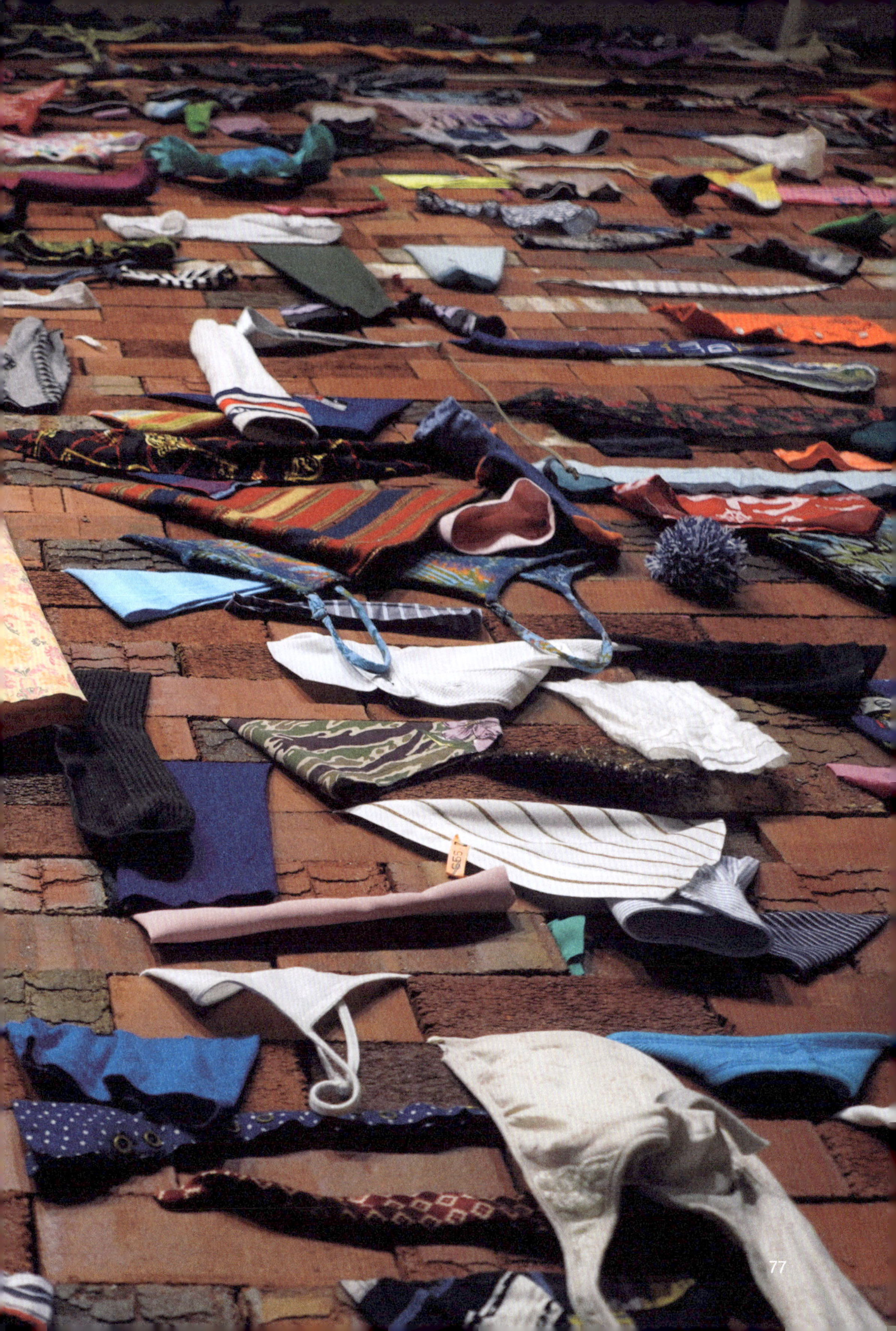

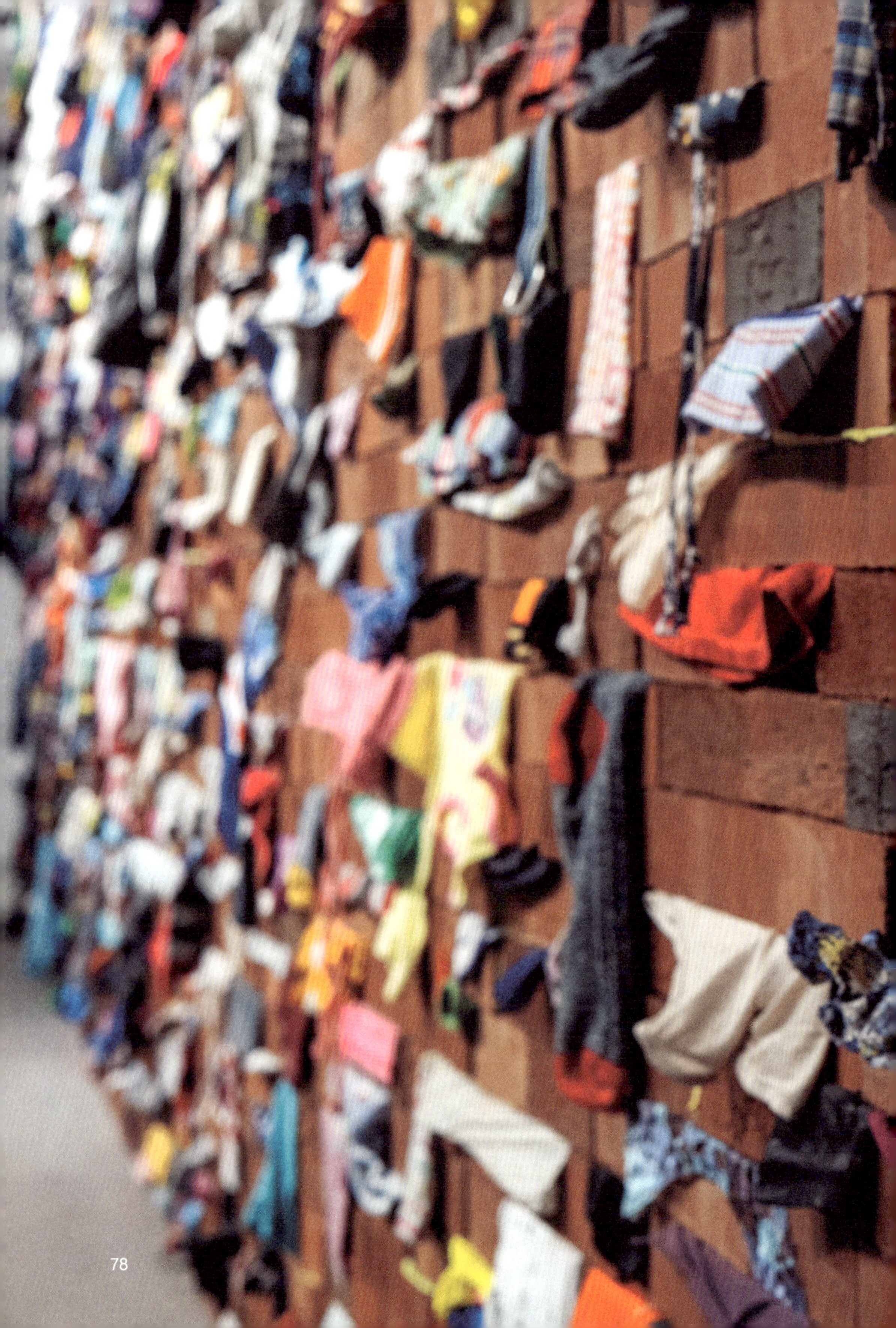

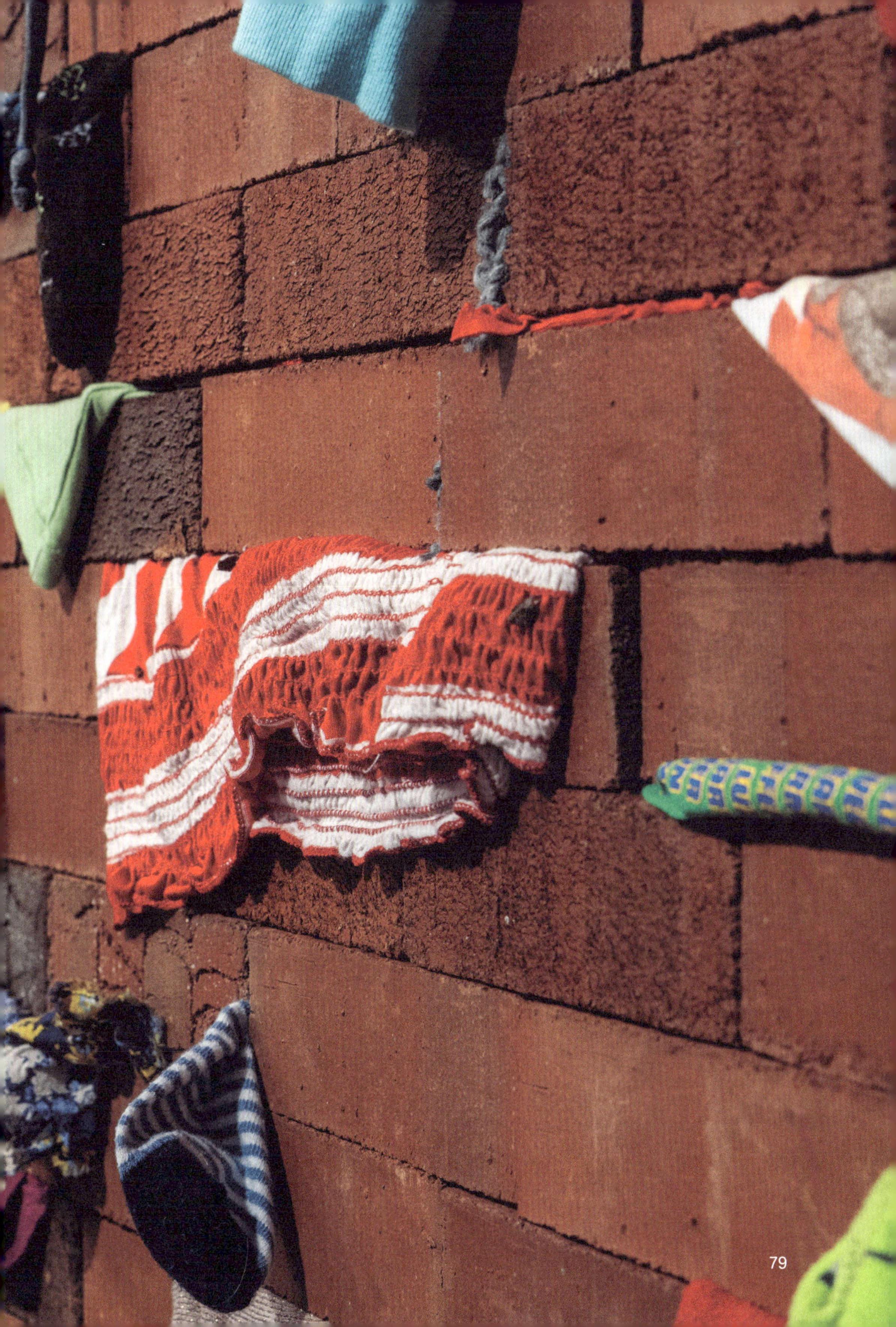

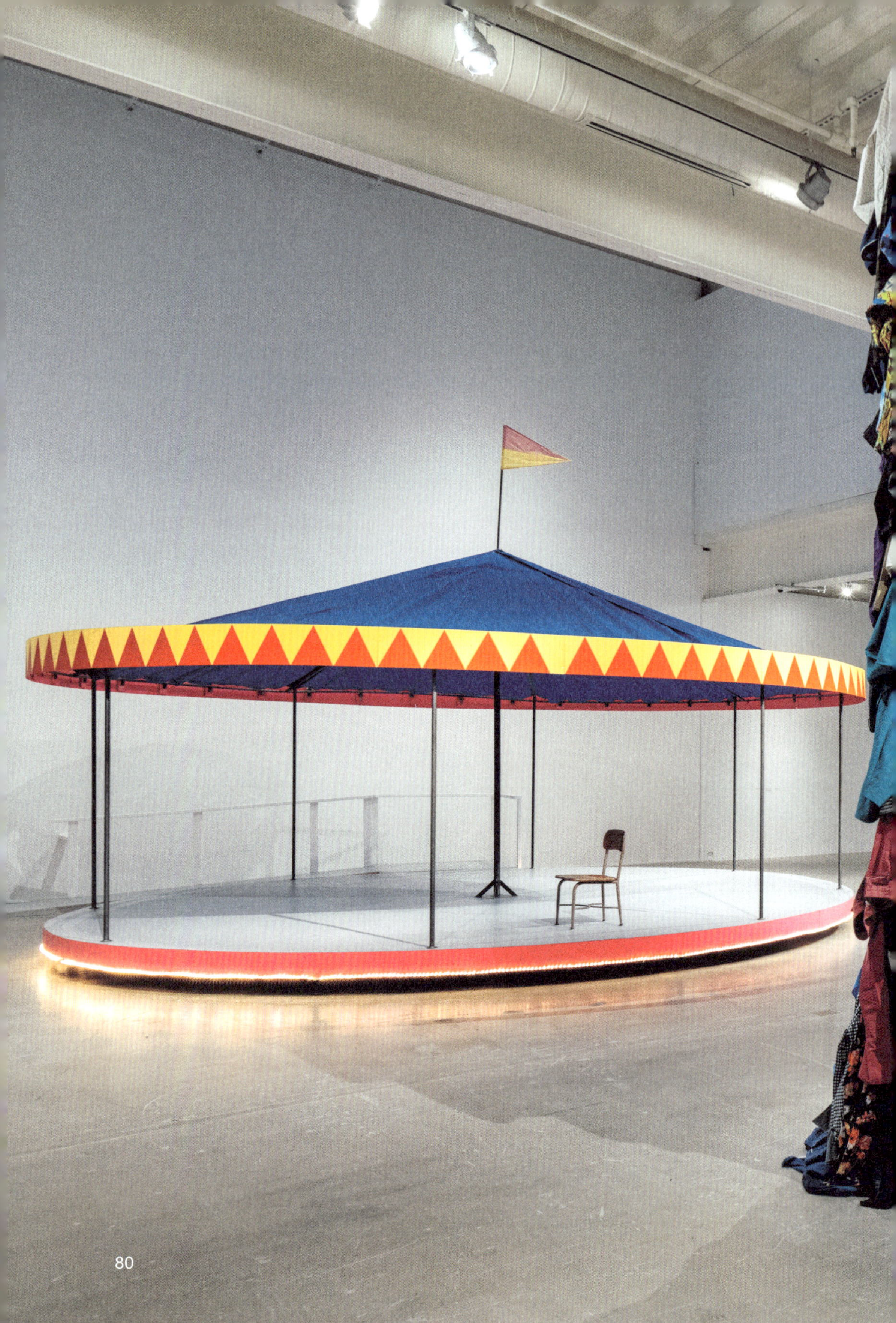

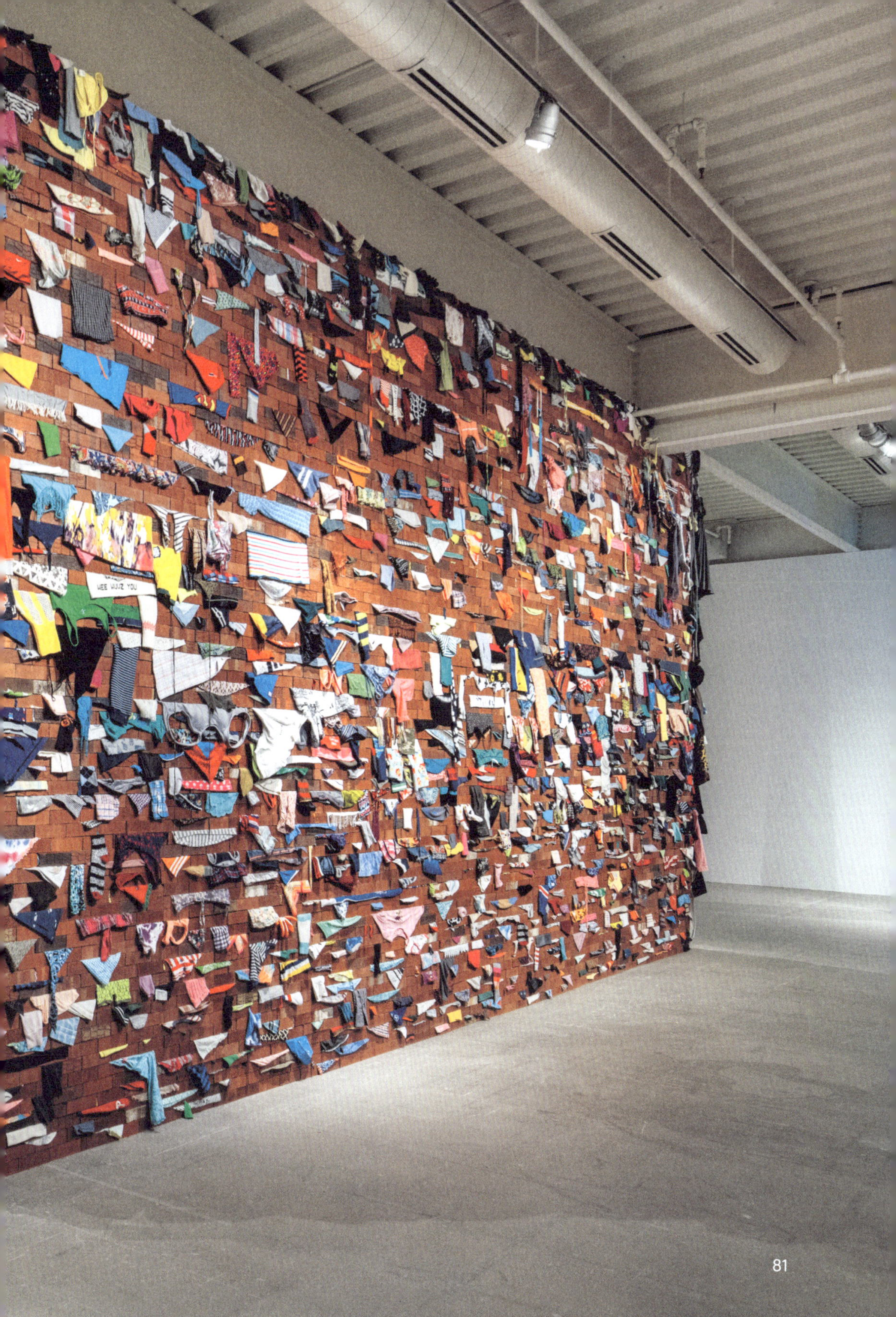

WEE WUZ YOU

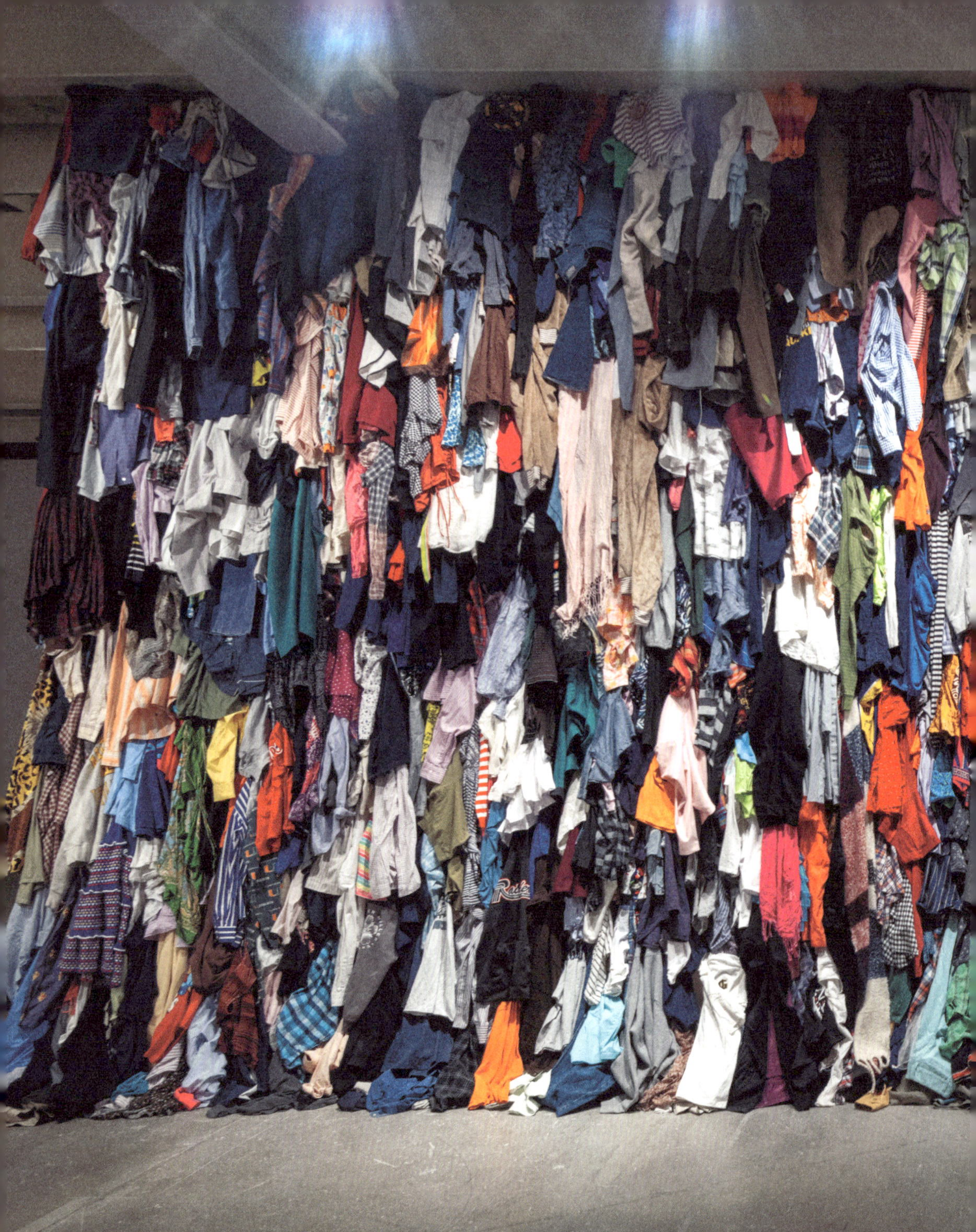

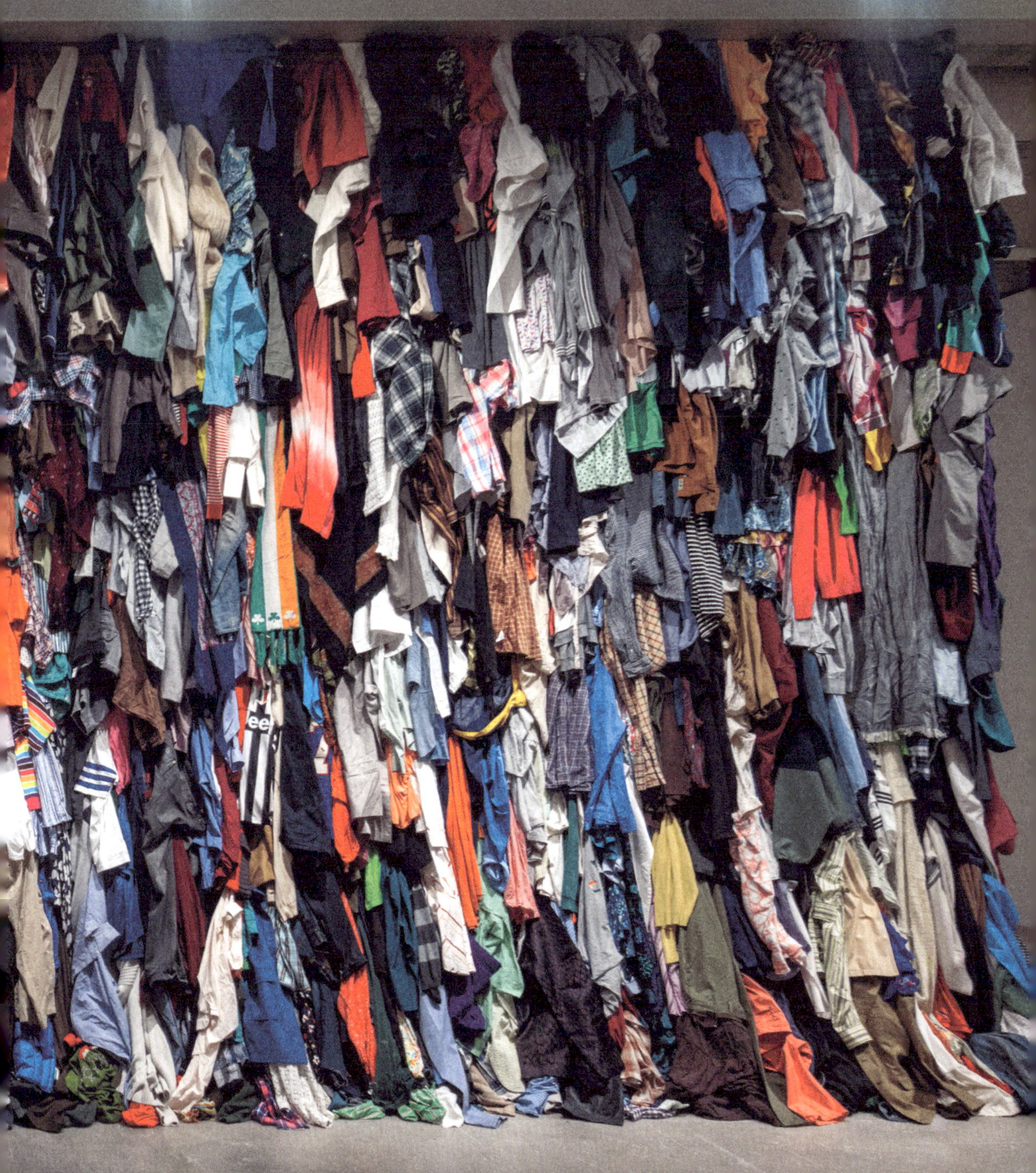

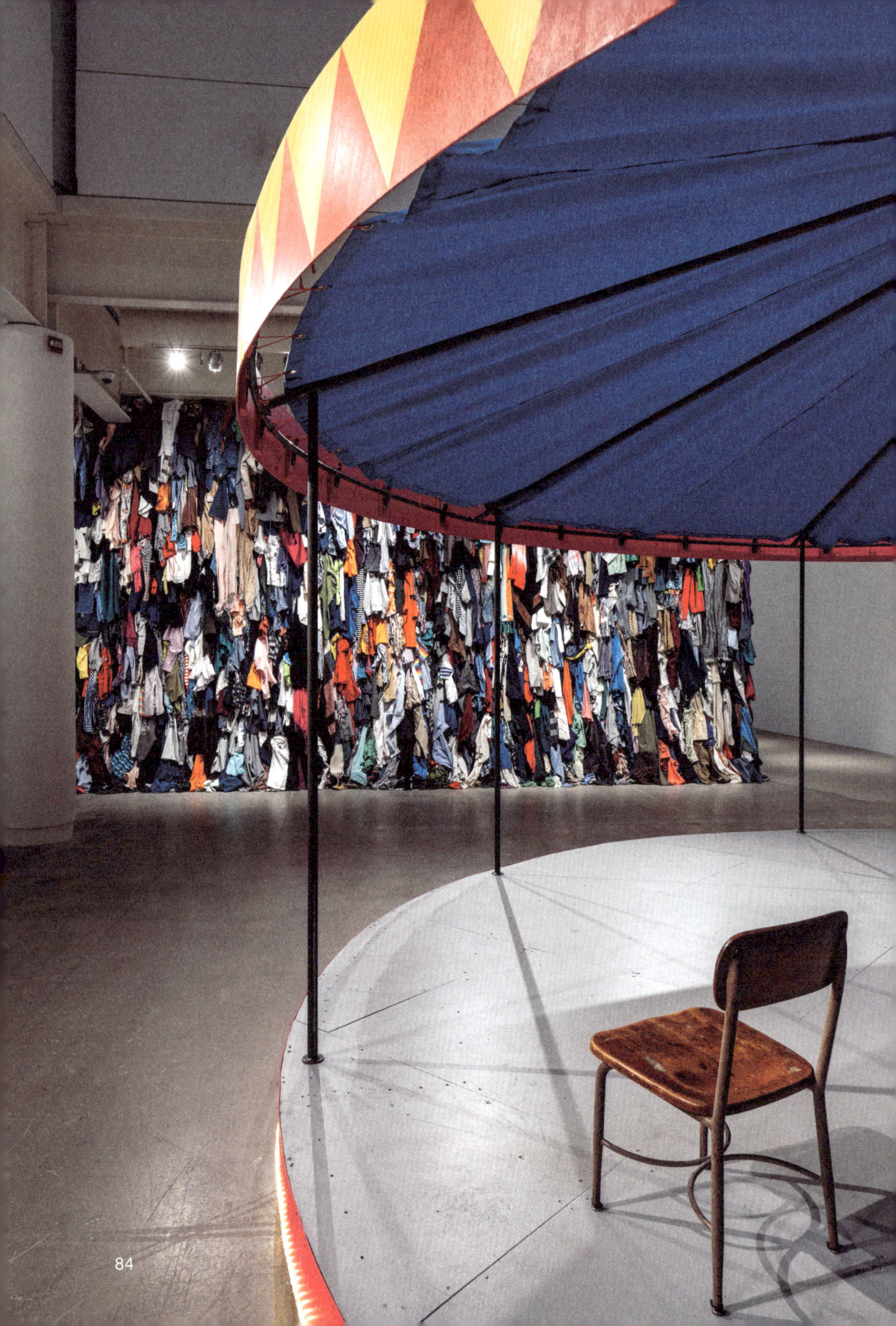

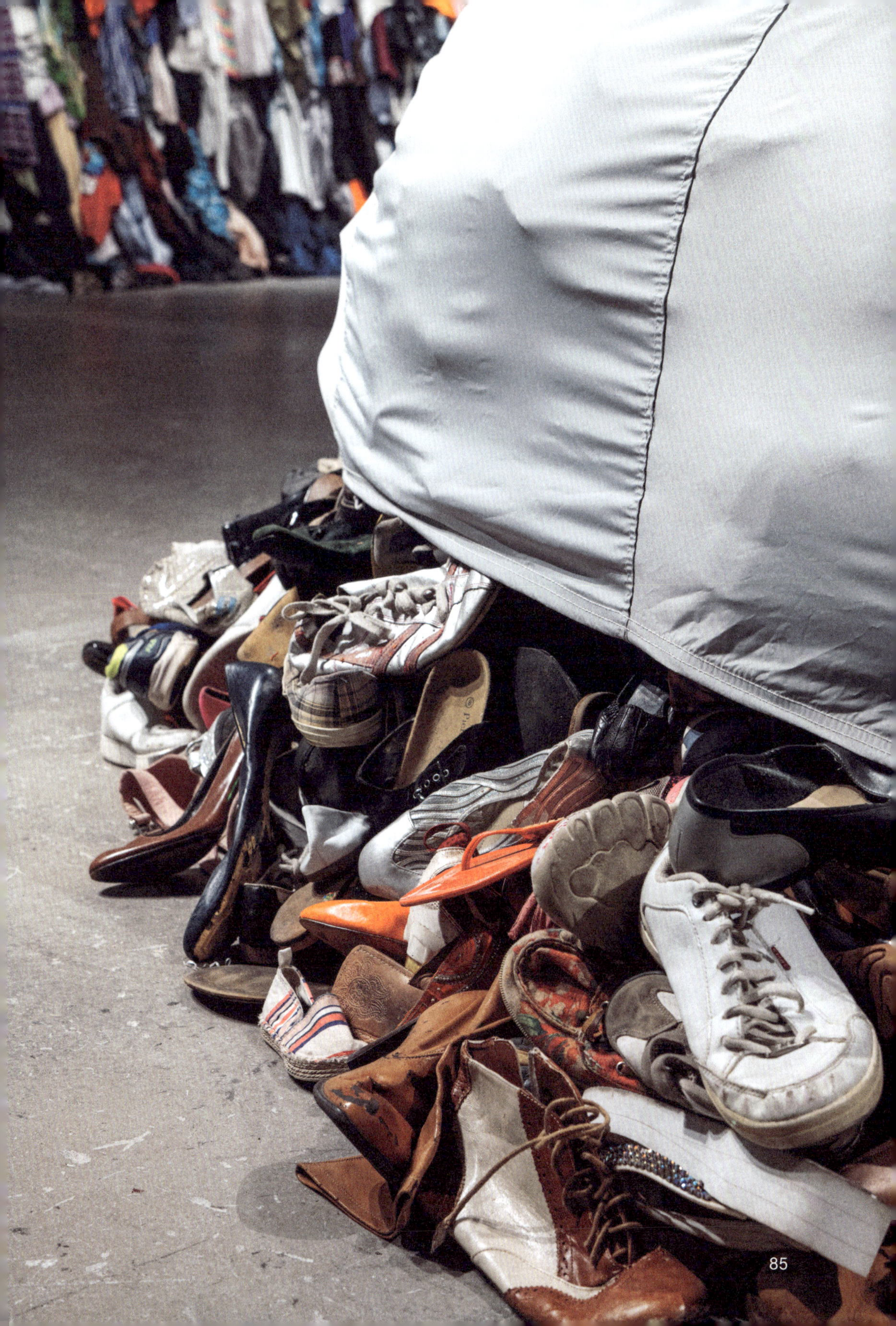

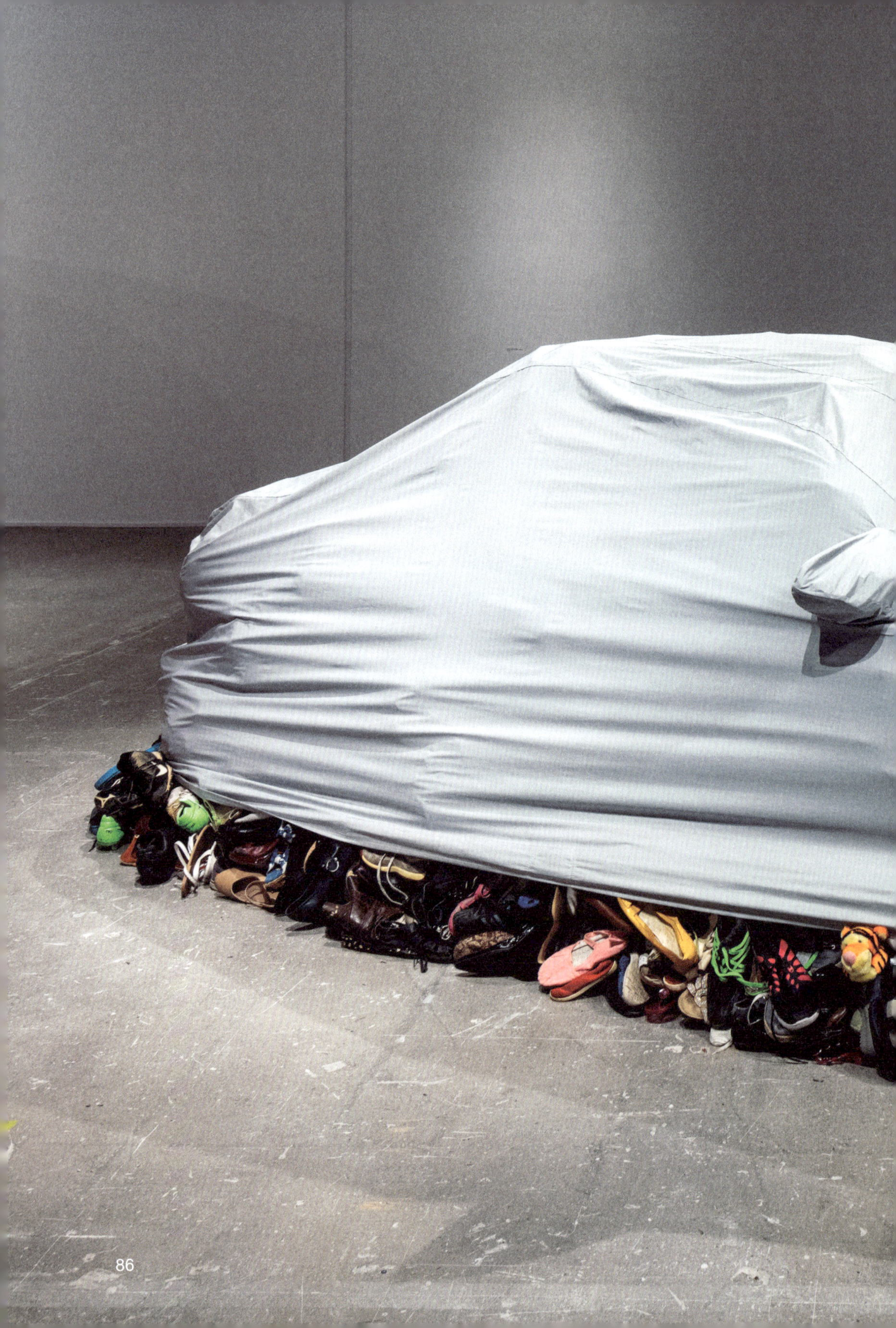

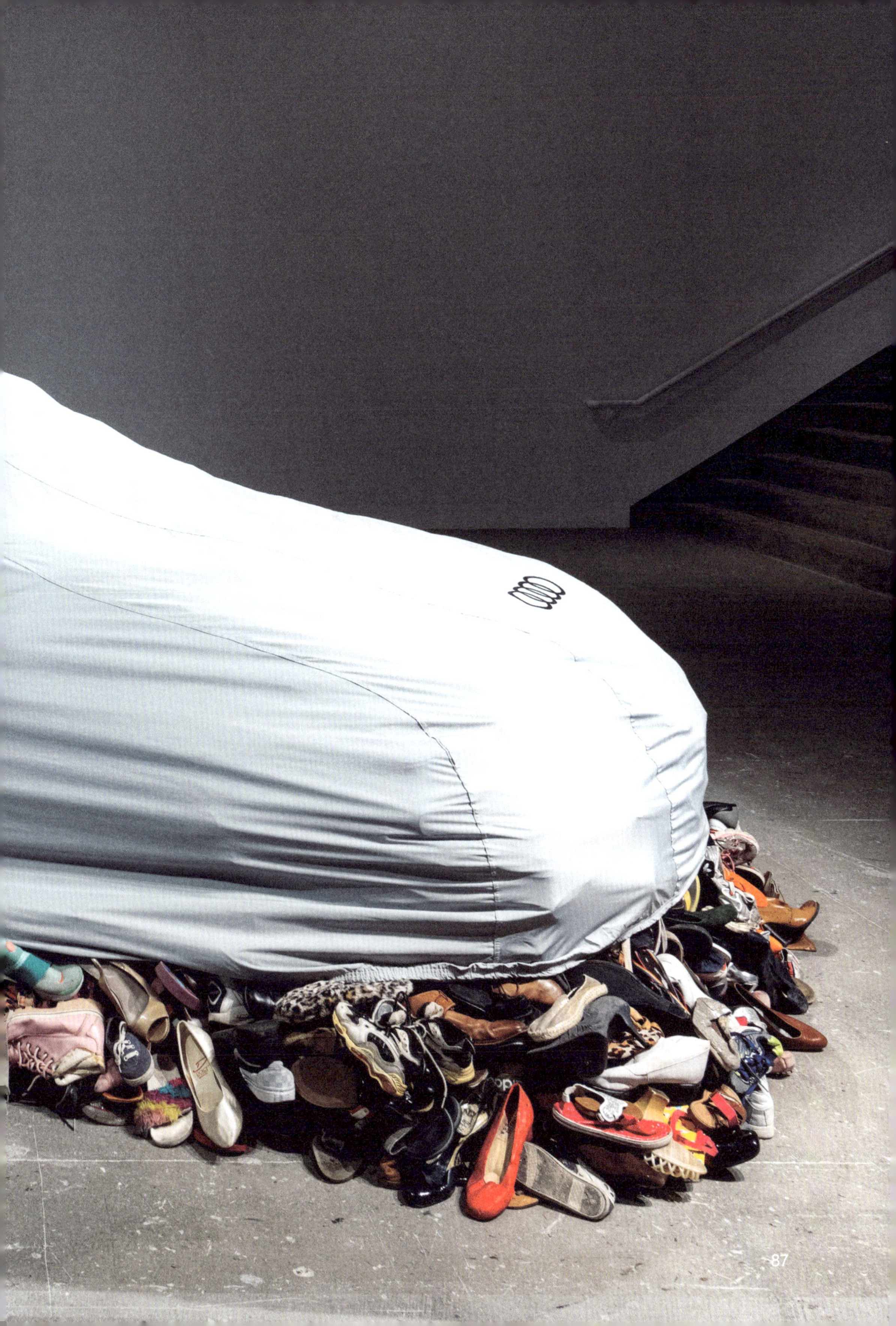

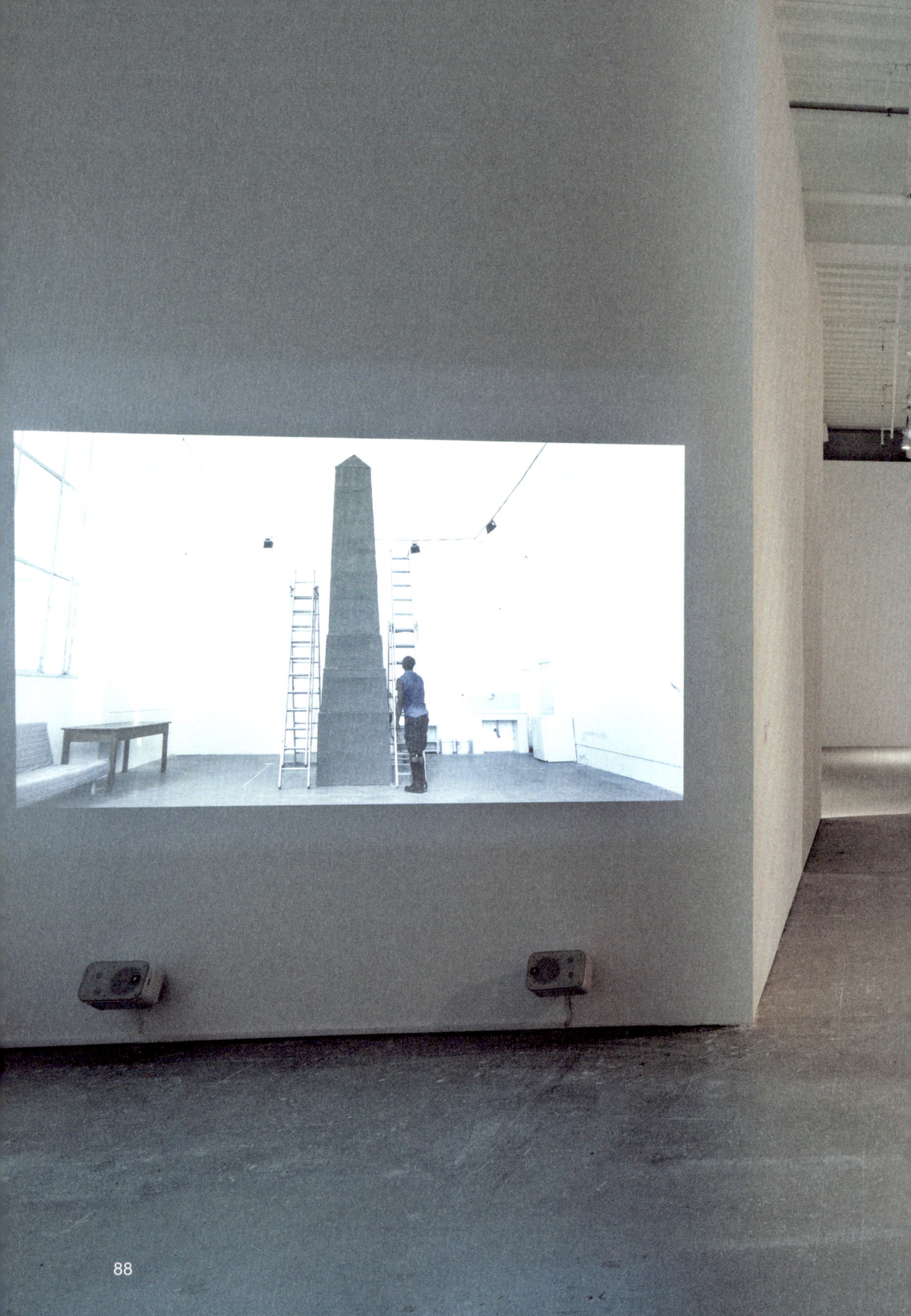

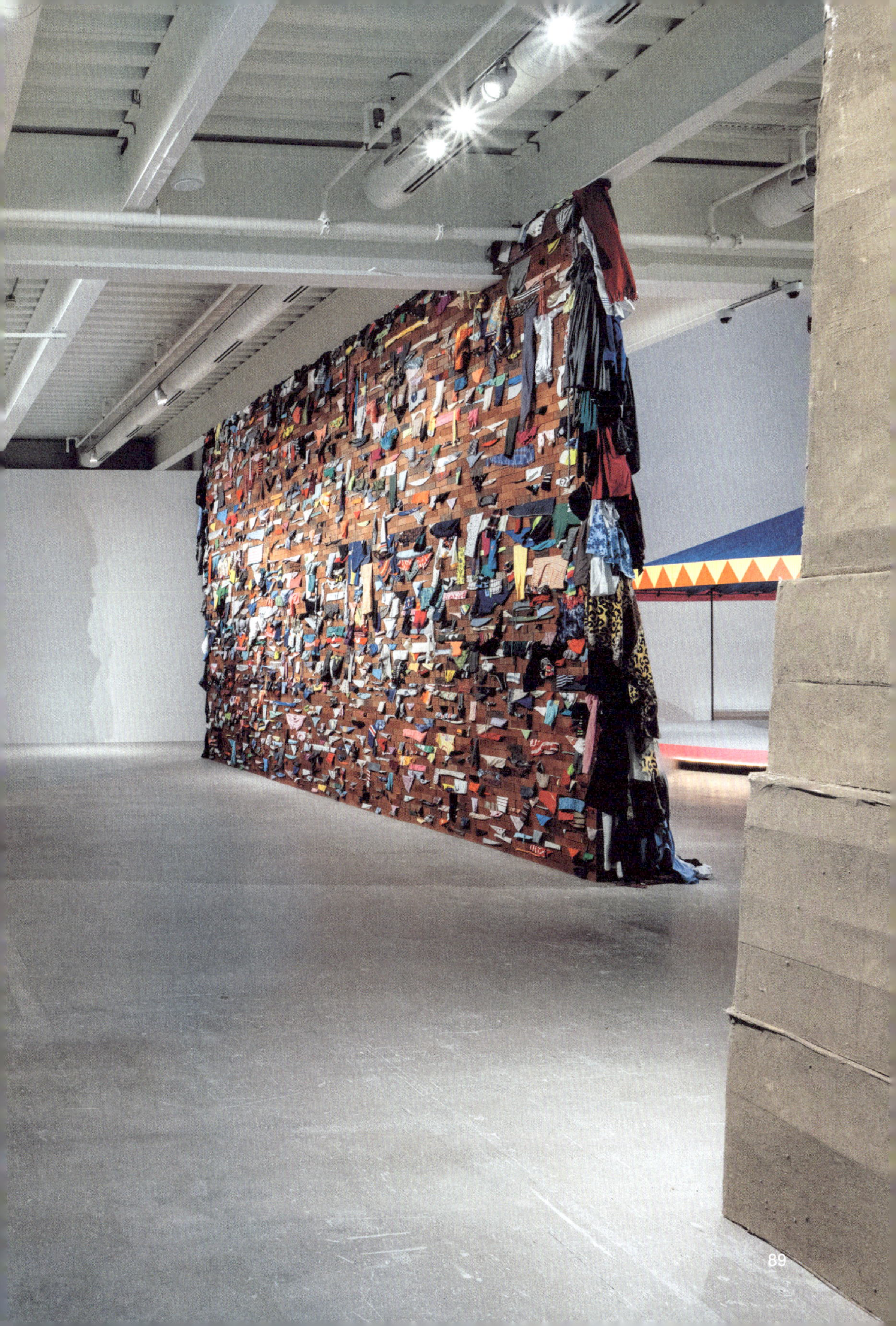

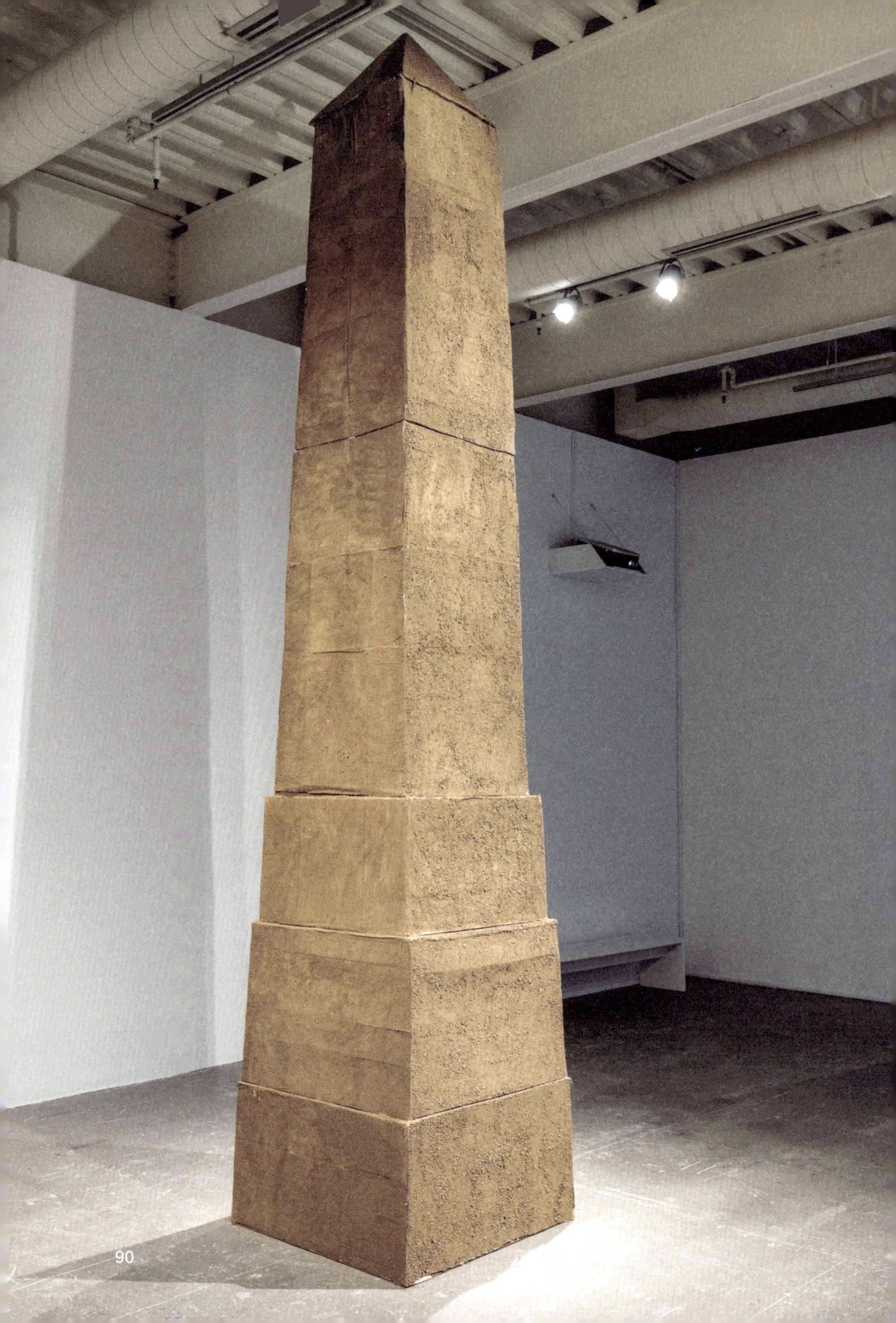

Moving the Obelisk, 2019–2020
cardboard, dirt, wood, tape, glue, hardware,
and single-channel color video, sound
12 minutes
Courtesy of the artist and Tanya Bonakdar Gallery,
New York / Los Angeles.

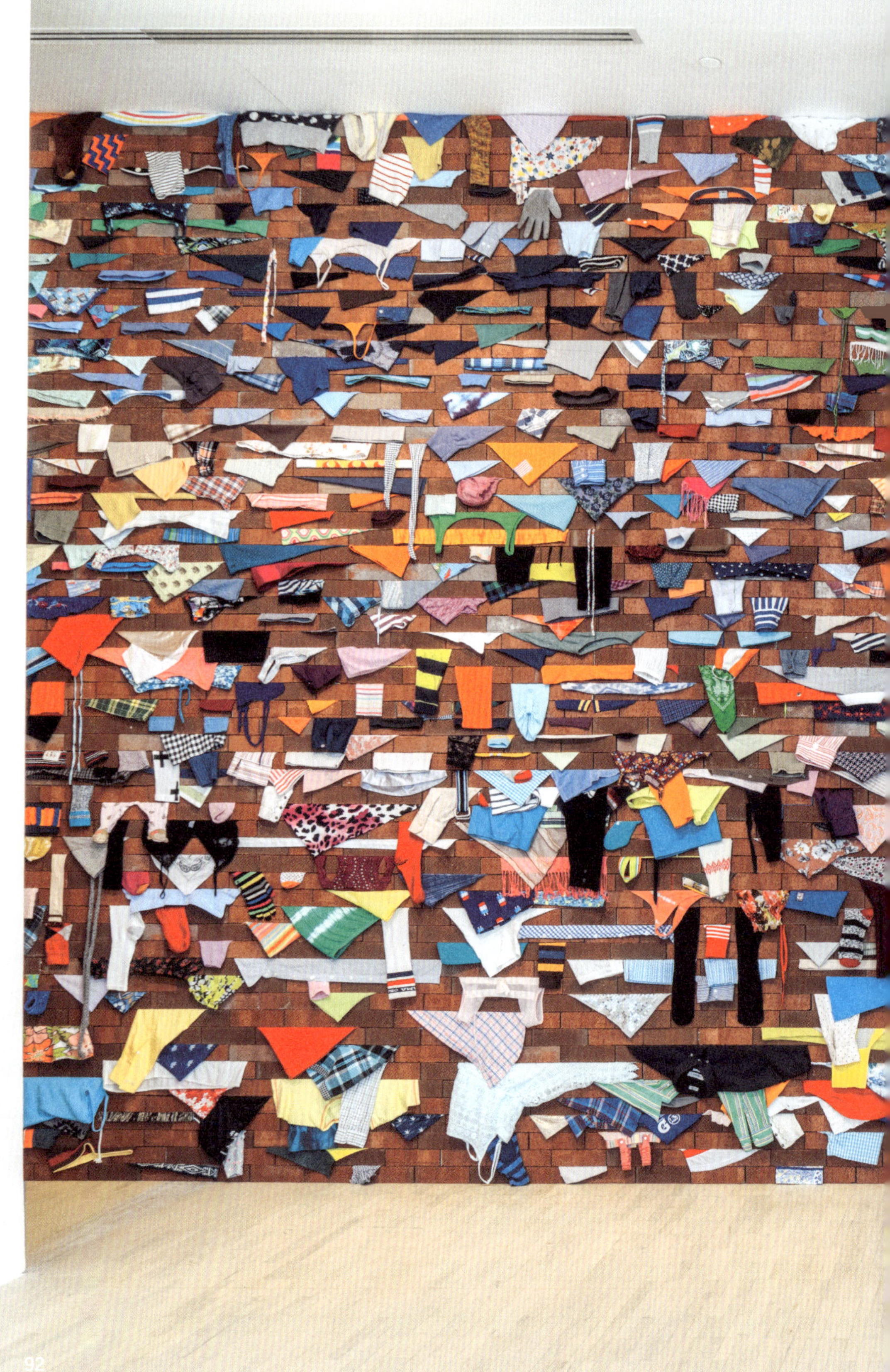

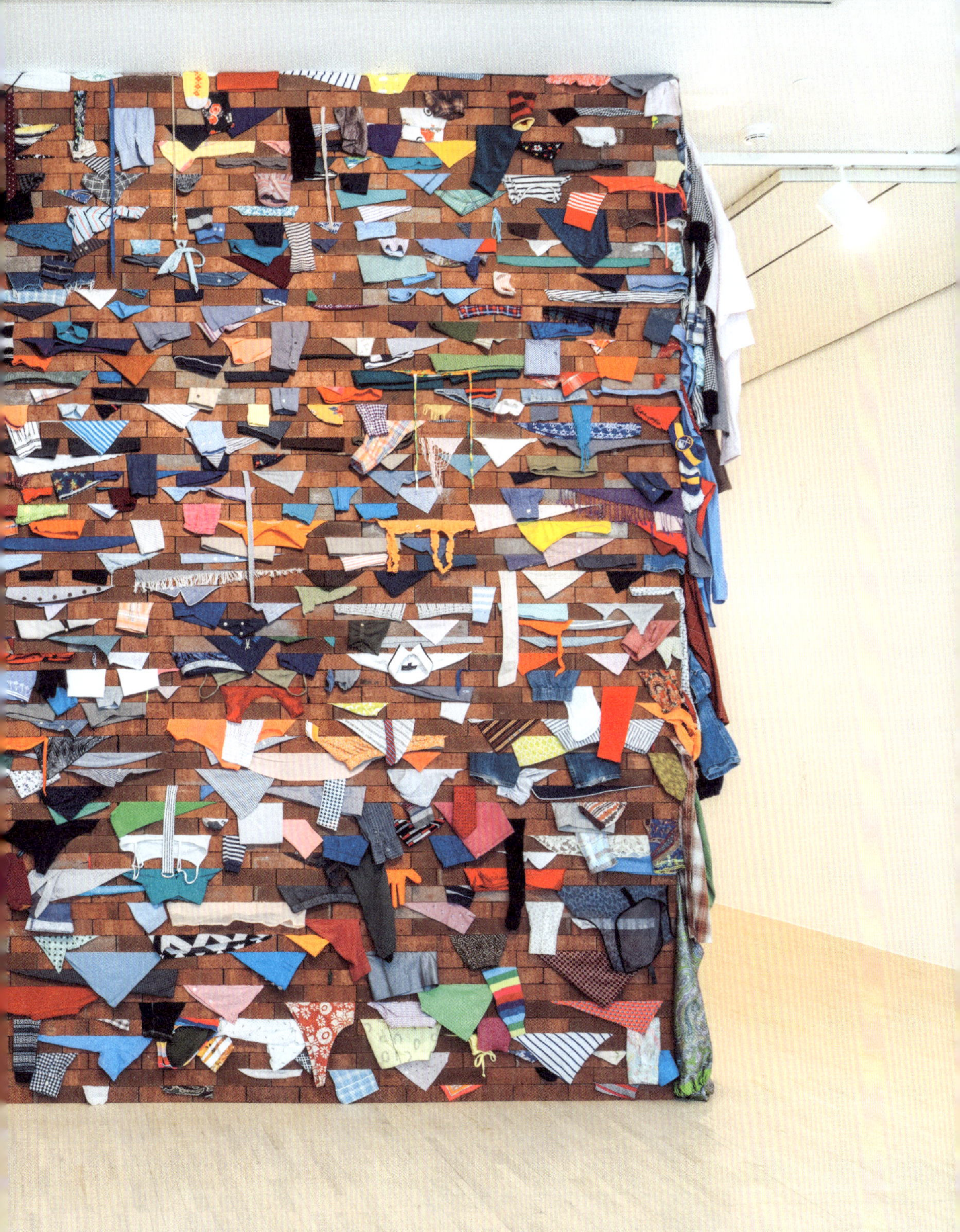

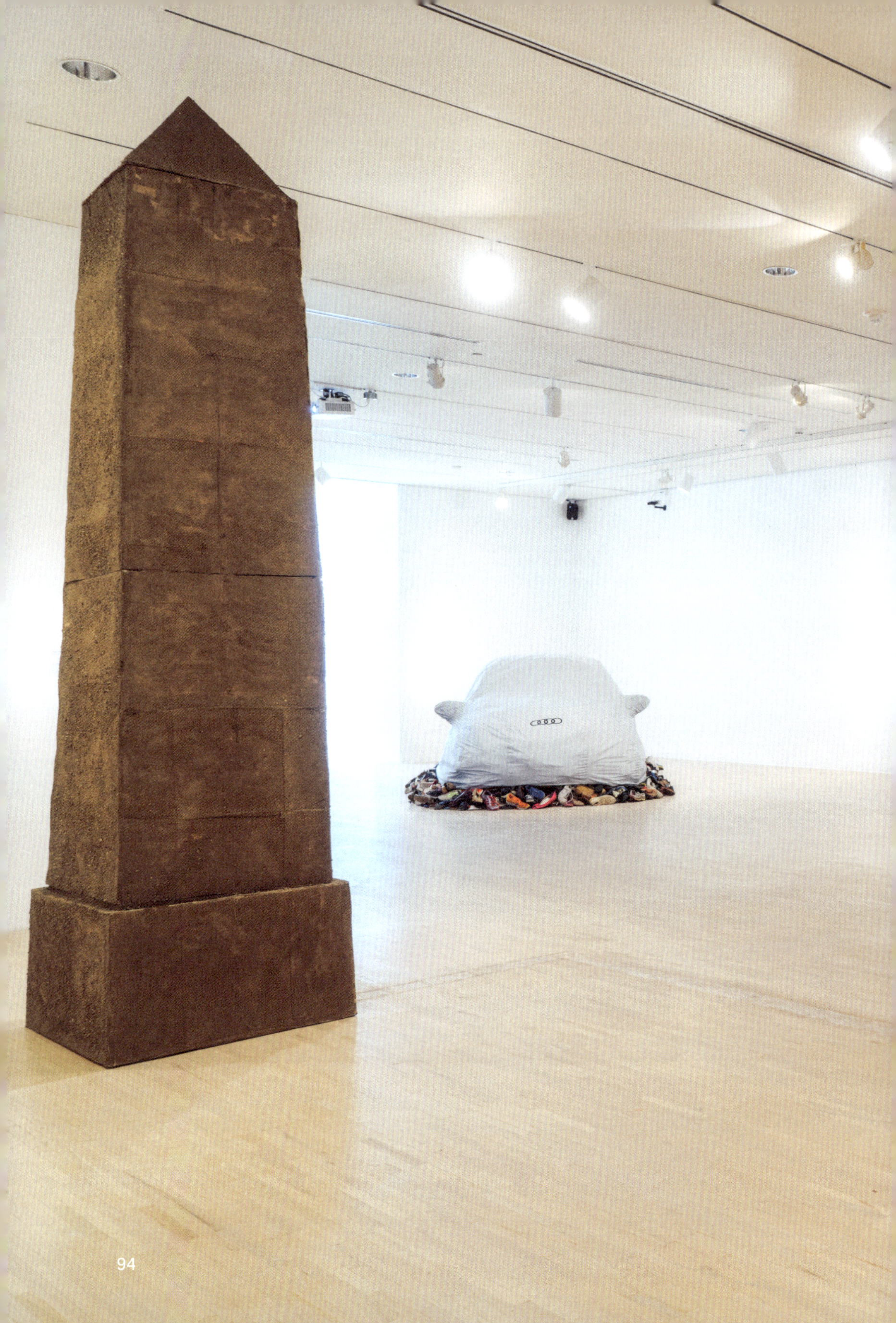

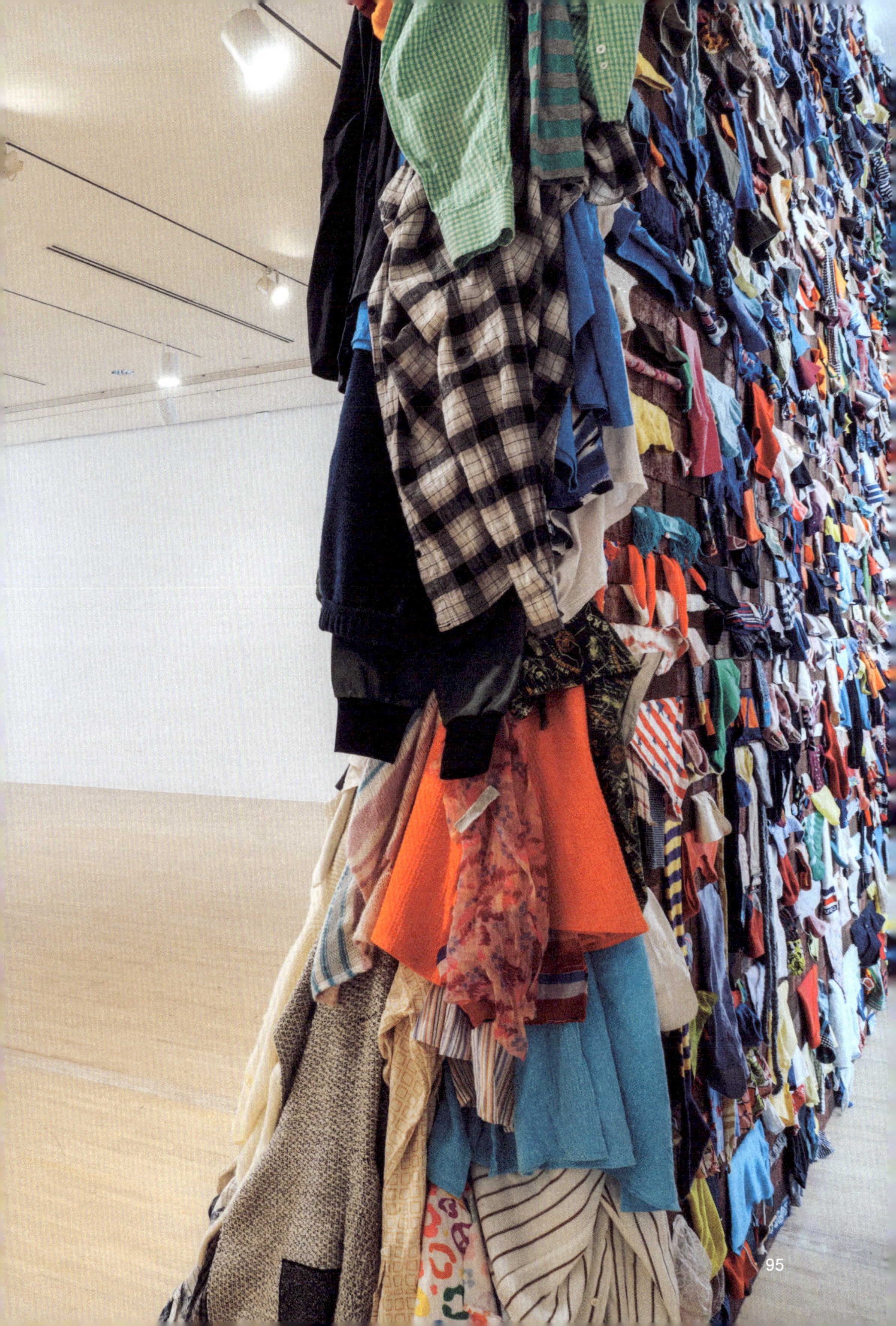

Winter Hung To Dry, 2003
UB Art Galleries
Used winter clothing and line
Dimensions variable
Courtesy of the artist and Tanya Bonakdar Gallery,
New York / Los Angeles

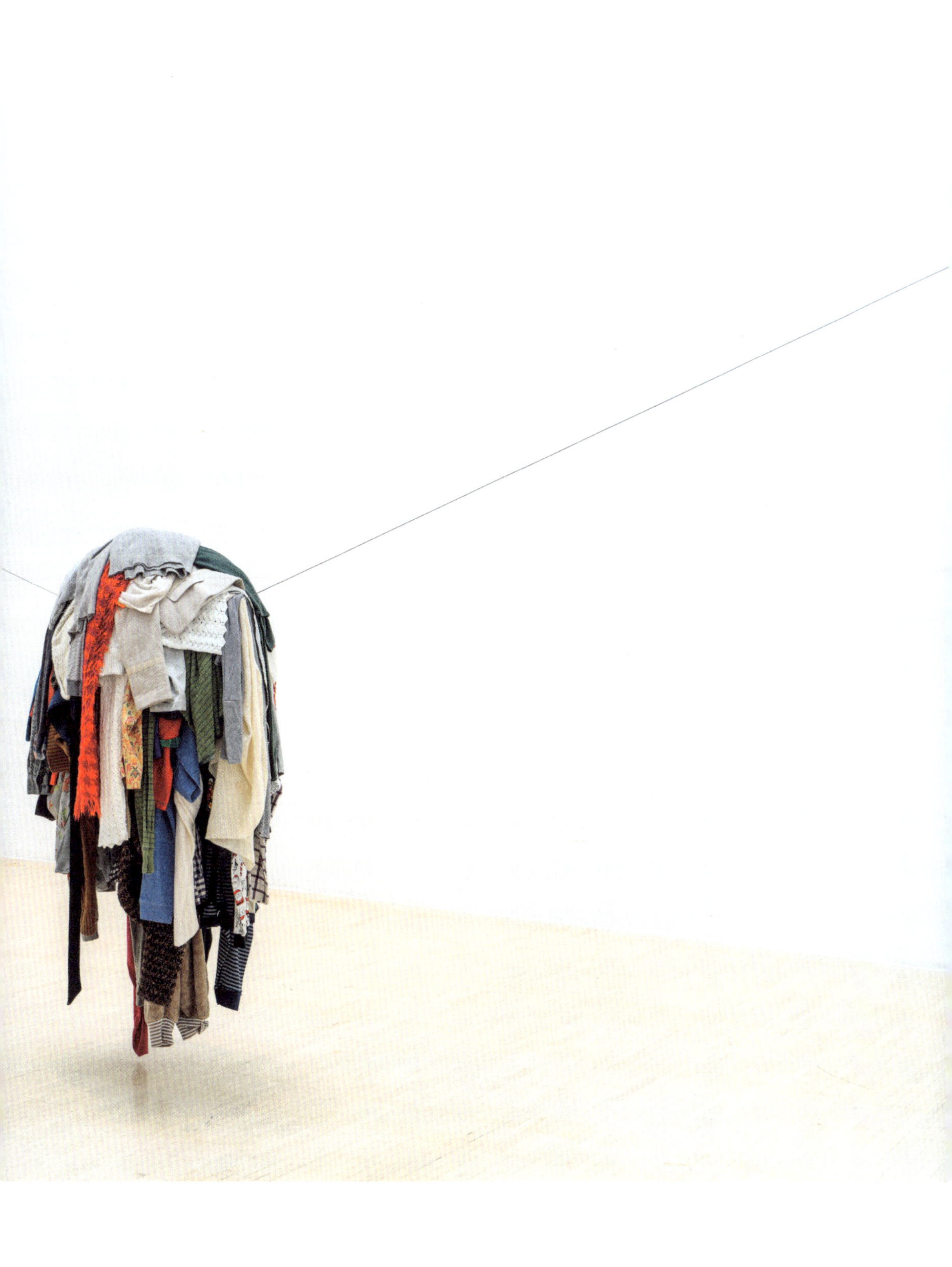

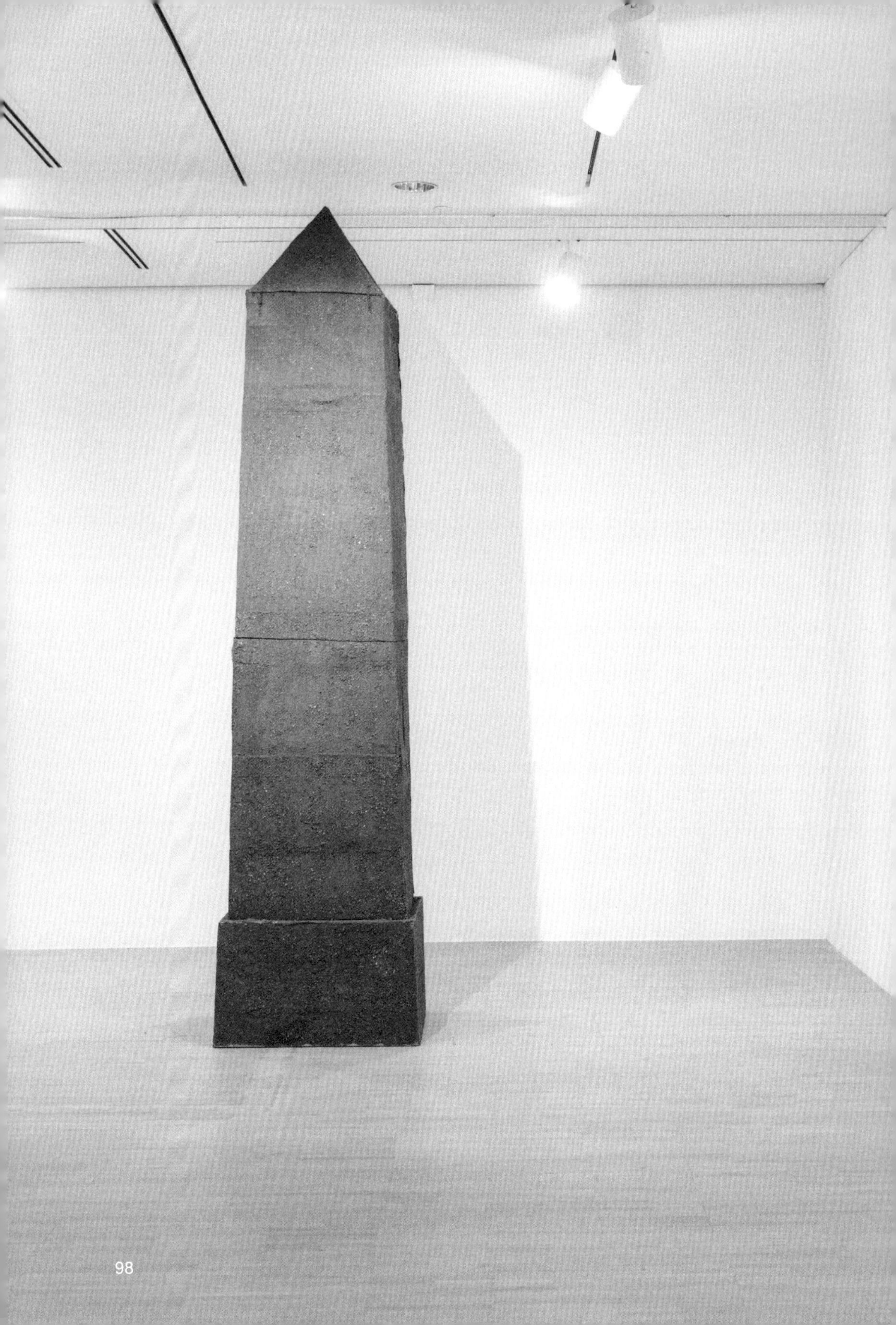

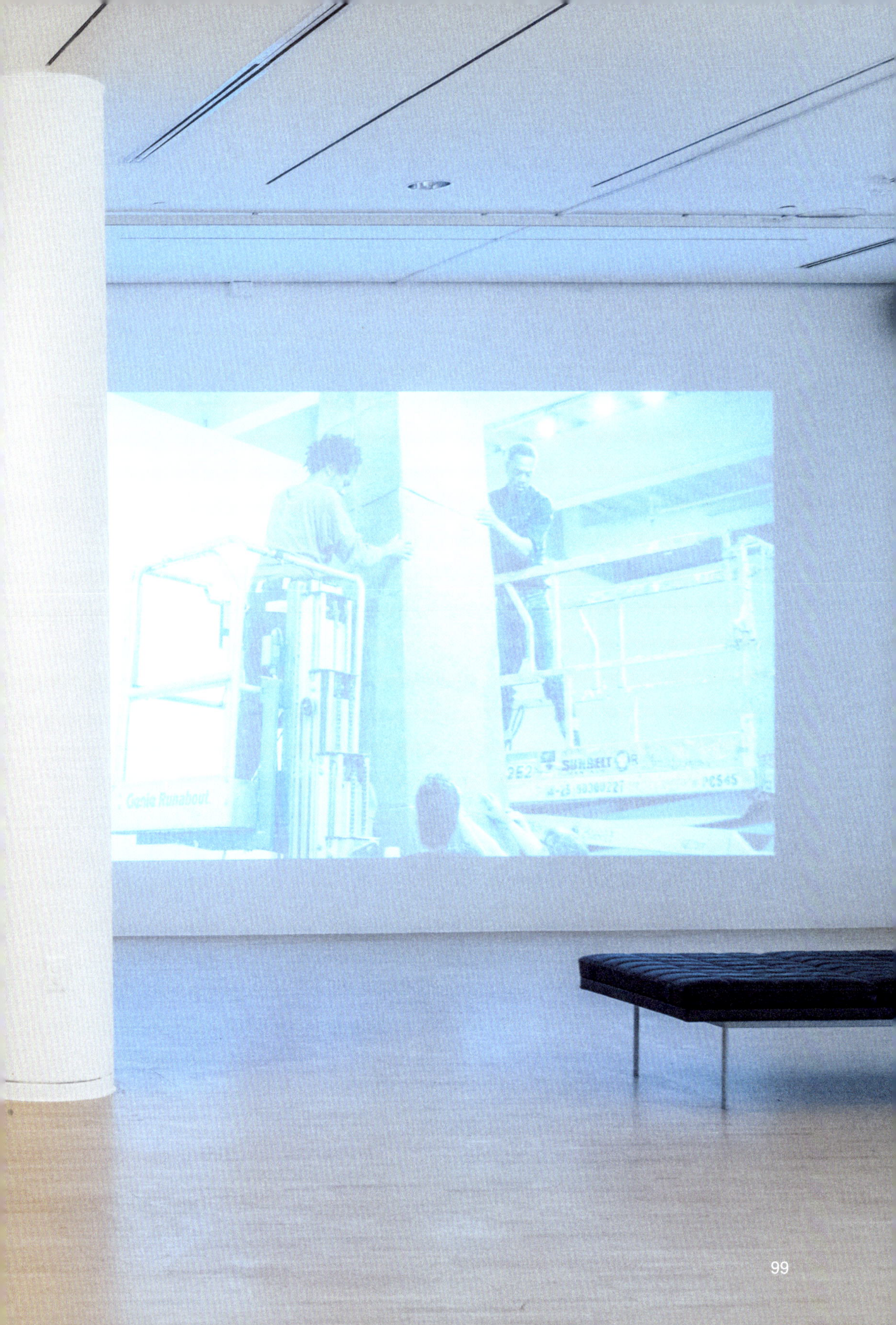

CHECKLIST

p 70–71
May 12, 1985, 2020
Carnations
Courtesy of the artist and Tanya Bonakdar Gallery,
New York / Los Angeles
(ICA installation only)

p 72–79, 81, 92–93, 95
Fortified, 2018–2020
Bricks, used clothing, and steel
Dimensions variable
Courtesy of the artist and Tanya Bonakdar Gallery,
New York / Los Angeles

p 80, 84
It's Not Over 'Til It's Over, 2004
Steel, wood, fabric, rope lighting,
rotating floor, and chair
14 × 24 ft. diameter
Courtesy of the artist and Tanya Bonakdar Gallery,
New York / Los Angeles
(ICA installation only)

p 85, 86–87, 94
Car Cover and Export Shoes, 2018
Car cover, expired shoes, and support materials
15.5 × 6 × 4.5 ft.
Courtesy of the artist and Tanya Bonakdar Gallery,
New York / Los Angeles

Summoned, 2020
Sound installation, recording of noon bells from
San Giovanni Crisostomo in Giuliano di Lecce, Italy
Courtesy of the artist and Tanya Bonakdar Gallery,
New York / Los Angeles

p 88, 89, 90–91, 94, 98–99
Moving the Obelisk, 2019–2020
Cardboard, dirt, wood, tape, glue, hardware,
and single-channel color video, sound
12 minutes
Courtesy of the artist and Tanya Bonakdar Gallery,
New York / Los Angeles

p 96–97
Winter Hung To Dry, 2003
Used winter clothing and line
Dimensions variable
Courtesy of the artist and Tanya Bonakdar Gallery,
New York / Los Angeles
(UB Art Galleries installation only)

How to Move a Monument

LIZ PARK

PART I:
MONUMENT

In 2018–2019, Trinidadian-born, Philadelphia-based artist Karyn Olivier wandered the streets of the Eternal City to study public art as per her successful proposal to the American Academy in Rome, Italy. Olivier wrote in her application, "I will identify… ten to twenty public works/sites over the eleven-month fellowship and create a proposal or prototype that is in conversation with the original. For each, I will make a model. These models will take different forms—fabricated sculpture, installation, 2D image, prose, or a video piece—and will function as finished artworks."[1] A hallowed environment for the study and advancement of art of all disciplines, the Academy provided Olivier almost a year of uninterrupted research amid the abundance of architectural and sculptural monuments of wildly ranging epochs. During her time in Rome, Olivier's proposal narrowed in focus. Rather than construct ten to twenty models of public artworks, the artist identified and dug deep into a particular form: the obelisk. Of ancient Egyptian, not Roman, origin, the obelisk appealed in its simplicity of form and complexity of histories.

"An obelisk. Comprised of a square, tapering shaft, and a pyramidion of 60 degrees at its top. Monolithic, excavated. Made from one solid stone; usually granite. The Greeks called them *obeliskos*, but the ancient Egyptian named them *tekhen*, taken from the verb meaning 'to pierce'," writes Olivier, for the voice-over narration in the twelve-minute video component of her 2020 work *Moving the Obelisk*.[2] "It's common knowledge that Rome now has more erect obelisks than anywhere else, including Egypt, homeland of the obelisk," she continues. The artist consulted *Moving the Obelisks: A Chapter in Engineering History in which the Vatican Obelisk in Rome in 1586 was*

---

1   "Karyn Olivier," Rome Prize Fellows, American Academy in Rome, accessed August 30, 2020, https://www.aarome.org/people/rome-prize-fellows/karyn-olivier.

2   All quotes by Karyn Olivier are from the narration of her video *Moving the Obelisk* (2020) unless otherwise noted. The narration in the video is by Trapeta Mason, 2020–2021 Philadelphia Poet Laureate.

Moved by Muscle Power by Bern Dibner as part of her research.[3] The lengthy subtitle leaves little mystery as to the book's focus: what was involved in moving the monoliths, which often weighed hundreds of tons. It also underscores, importantly, the transportability of these monuments to power. In conquering Egypt in 30 BCE, the Roman Empire took liberty of repurposing the ancient religious symbol, pairs of which originally marked temple entrances. As lone, sky-piercing landmarks, displaced and strewn around the so-called Capital of the World—*Caput Mundi*—the obelisks signified the empire's might and reach. Four centuries later, Rome, too, would fall, but the obelisks would remain standing two millennia later to greet pilgrims to the capital of present-day Italy.

A culmination of the artist's immersion in this ancient city replete with such monoliths, *Moving the Obelisk* began as an exercise in building a provisional structure in drastic contrast to the grandiosity of the ancient Egyptian relics. Olivier assembled humble materials in her vaulted studio at the Academy. After fashioning the basic structure of an obelisk in segments using cardboard, wood, tape, and hardware, she covered it with dirt, freshly dug up from the Academy's garden, using a generous amount of glue. The final construction stood in her studio at an imposing height of eighteen feet. However, the completion of this hollow-yet-immense sculpture marked only the beginning of the work. Having fixed the crumbly Roman earth onto the equally brittle cardboard, Olivier next orchestrated a complex choreography that involved a camera crew, an informal team of art handlers, and a professional art packing and shipping company.

The artist directed a video shoot of herself and a team of helpers gingerly dismantling the obelisk, segment by segment. In the video, she is seen laying the unwieldy sculpture horizontally on the studio floor, then measuring the length of the shaft multiple times before cutting it into pieces with a small, handheld saw blade. The cut

3 Bern Dibner, *Moving the Obelisks: A Chapter in Engineering History in which the Vatican Obelisk in Rome in 1586 was Moved by Muscle Power, and a Study of More Recent Similar Moves* (Cambridge: MIT, 1970).

pieces are then stored inside other hollow segments of the obelisk, like Russian nesting dolls. Then come the art shippers in matching uniforms, carefully wrapping the nested cardboard segments in plastic and placing them in two large crates. The crates are expertly handled and loaded onto a truck and, in the last bit of the footage shot in Rome, the truck is seen driving away. The scene ends here.

This was July 2019, the conclusion of Olivier's Italian sojourn. Upon return to her home and studio in the Germantown neighborhood of Philadelphia, the artist set to work on her upcoming solo exhibition at the Institute of Contemporary Art at the University of Pennsylvania in January 2020, where *Moving the Obelisk* was set to make its debut. She revisited older works—three of which she chose to present in the ICA exhibition—and the meanings that they have shed and accumulated over the years. To organize her thoughts, she scribbled shared attributes among these works and the yet-to-be-completed *Moving the Obelisk* on a piece of paper: move(ment); transportation; cross Atlantic/Mediterranean; crossing borders; mortality (spoils of water); LABOR; displacement; haptic; monument; memory; temporal. So read the column of words under "Moving the Obelisk." The older works she was thinking through included: *It's Not Over 'Til It's Over* (2004)—a slow moving carousel furnished with an ordinary chair for the lone rider; *Car Cover and Export Shoes* (2018)—a sculpture in the shape of an automobile with old shoes stuffed under a luxury car cover; and *Fortified* (2018–2020)—a brick wall with secondhand clothes peeking out in place of grout. Under the title of each work, Olivier jotted with consistency: movement, move, move (ment), displaced(ment), displacement, memorial (of sorts), monumental, monument/memorial. The thread in this exercise became clear. Just as the ancient Romans understood the power in mobilizing a monument across the Mediterranean Sea, Olivier understood that the contemporary relevance of her makeshift obelisk was rooted in its trans-Atlantic crossing to the United States, where, in a gallery, it would stand as both art and witness to present-day global transportation network that made possible its very existence.

Karyn Olivier's notebook, 2019

car cover w/export shoes	wallet/ clothes	moving the obelisk
move(ment)	move(ment)	move
transportation	transportation	transportation
cross Atlantic		cross Atlantic/ mediterranean
Border crossing	Border crossing	Crossing Borders
mortality (refugee/migrant)	mortality (migrant)	mortality (spoils of war)
LABOR	LABOR	LABOR
displacement	displacement	displacement
cyclical		
haptic	haptic	haptic
monumental	monument memorial	monument
containment	containment	
absence	absence	
		memory
hidden	hidden	temporal
tactive		

Olivier's obelisk is a flimsy construction made out of cardboard shipping boxes. Her video even captures the smirking arrow—part of Amazon's logo—imprinted on a collapsed box. Rather than a solid piece of stone, the artist uses the detritus of neoliberal, multinational corporatism. The global reach of the online retail giant exemplifies contemporary consolidation of power that is as sweeping as that of ancient empires. The efficacy of the so-called e-commerce today is nonetheless dependent on the labor of the world's working class, even as the marketing language of convenience renders invisible the work of retrieving, packing, and delivering goods, let alone their manufacture and assembly. Convenience is achieved at the cost of inconvenience to others; movement for some is achieved at the cost of displacement of others. In Olivier's video, every act is a concerted display. The functionless object is imbued with the symbolic weight of the collective labor of the artist, her team, and the shipping company. Laid bare for all to witness, the video reveals even the unsightly underside of the cardboard obelisk.

To be precise, Olivier's sculpture is not an obelisk, since it is hollow. The imitation of form, however, is significant in its reference to Benito Mussolini's monument built in 1932. The leader of Italy's brutal Fascist regime from 1922 to 1943, Mussolini intentionally tapped into the ancient Roman lineage as a way to encourage national pride. It was no accident that he chose the obelisk—made of far more expensive Carrara marble rather than the customary granite—as the centerpiece of Rome's Foro Mussolini, a sports complex established as part of the Fascist campaign to promote physical fitness.[4]

---

4 For a general recounting of Mussolini's obelisk, see Brian A. Curran et al., *Obelisk: A History* (Cambridge: MIT, 2009), 290.

For a discussion of Fascist remnants in Italy, including the obelisk, see Ruth Ben-Ghiat, "Why Are so Many Fascist Monuments Still Standing in Italy?" *New Yorker*, October 5, 2017, https://www.newyorker.com/culture/culture-desk/why-are-so-many-fascist-monuments-still-standing-in-italy.

For additional information on Mussolini's obelisk, see Erin Blakemore, "Scholars Uncover Secret Message from Mussolini," *Smithsonian Magazine*, September 1, 2016, https://www.smithsonianmag.com/smart-news/scholars-uncover-secret-message-mussolini-180960312/.

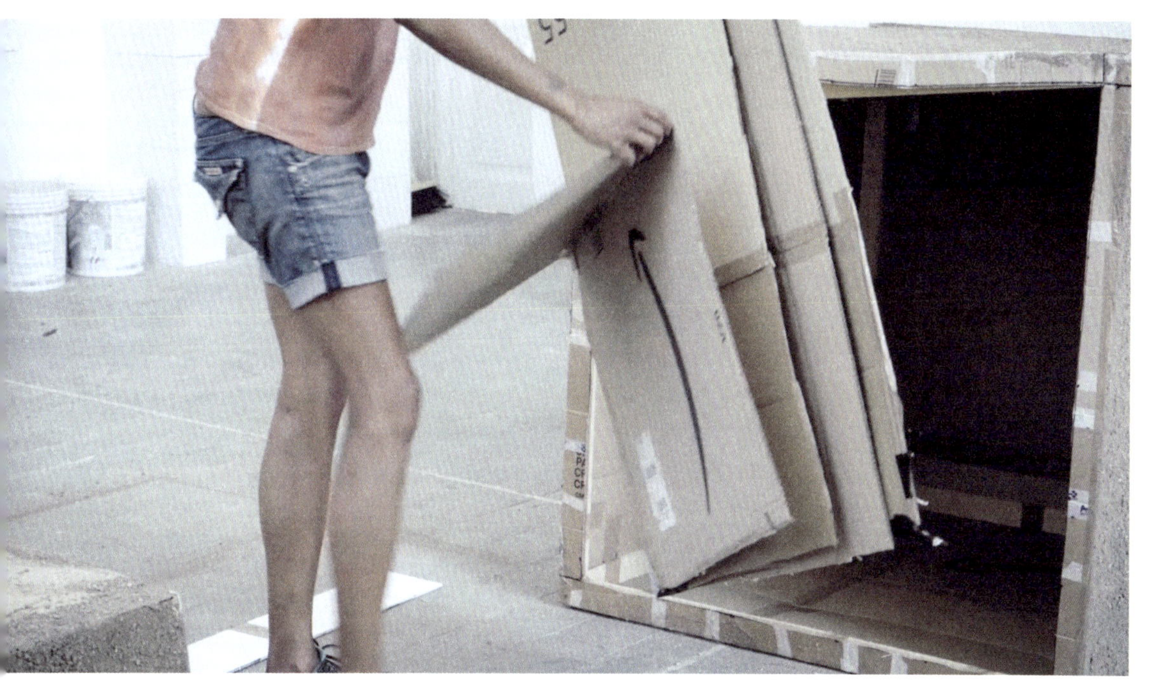

Moving the Obelisk, 2019–2020
Cardboard, dirt, wood, tape, glue, hardware, and single-channel color video, sound
12 minutes
Courtesy of the artist and Tanya Bonakdar Gallery, New York / Los Angeles

Although Foro Mussolini is now renamed Foro Italico, the glistening white marble obelisk with the golden point on the pyramidion still bears the words "MUSSOLINI DUX"–Latin for Mussolini the Leader. This piercing monument continues to broadcast his familiar honorific *Il Duce*. Coupled with the horrifying magnetism of Fascist relics in general and other pilgrimage sites such as Mussolini's tomb, this monolith still stands, demanding its place in a burdened history.

"This hollow shell is not really an obelisk, by definition," Olivier admits in her script for the video. "But what of the weight of emptiness? Its total weight, dispersed along its body, is probably close to my own. The cardboard, the dirt–similar in color. Similar to me in hue." Using her own brown-toned body as a standard of measure, the artist ponders the weight of emptiness. The emptiness of her obelisk mocks the solidity of Mussolini's monument. Olivier has symbolically emptied out the magnetic core of the Fascist monument. While emptiness cannot invert the weight of Fascist history, nor any history of conquest and pillage, it presents the potential for a new reading of the hollowed form.

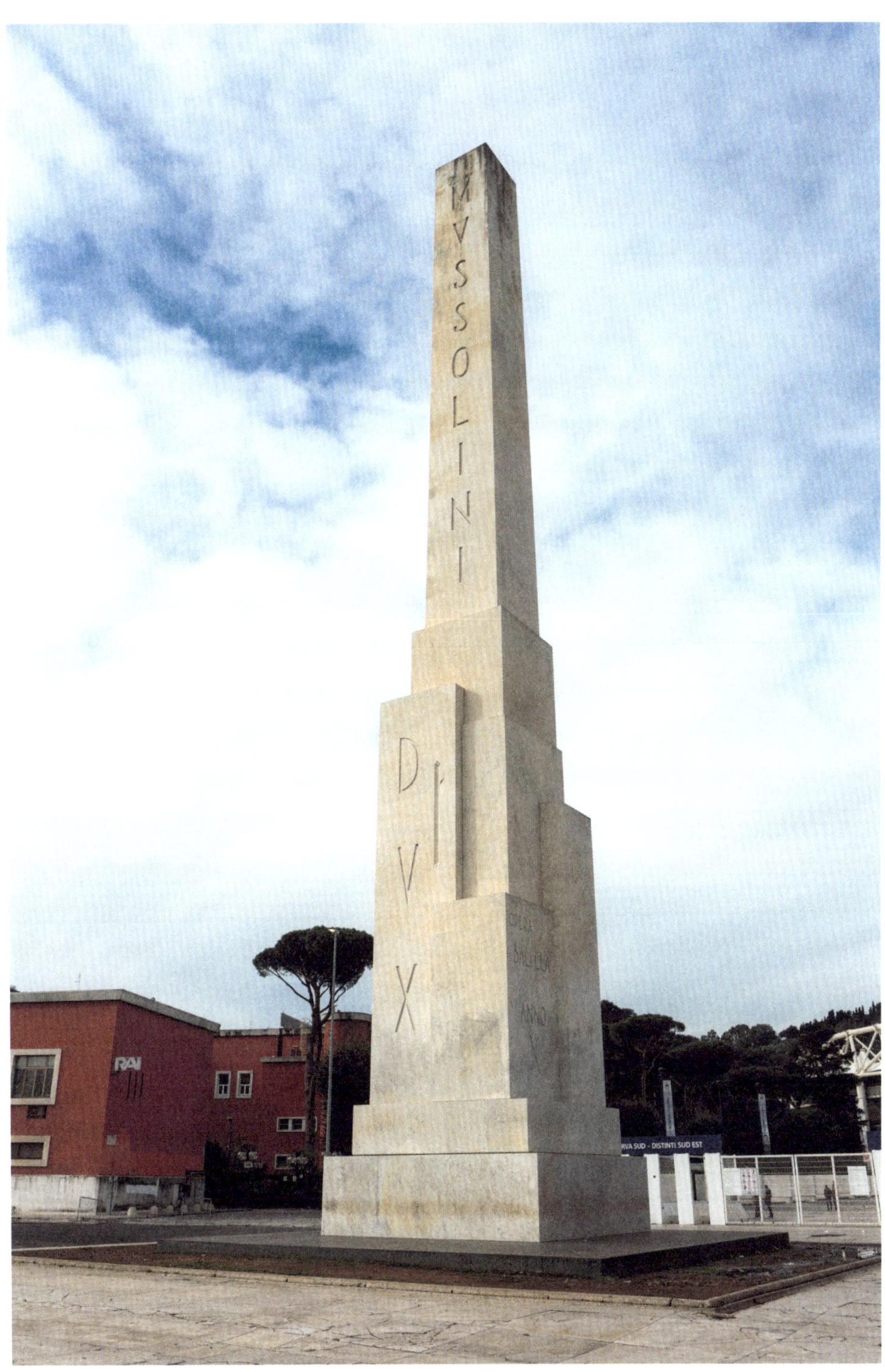

Rome, Italy. Obelisk at the entrance to the Foro Italico, bearing the insciption "Mussolini Dux"

PART II:
MOVEMENT

When Olivier left the stacked and crated obelisk sculpture in storage in Italy, she did not anticipate that it would take her months to fundraise for its shipment to Philadelphia. Art objects are subject to the same laws that govern economics and physics; objects at rest stay at rest unless acted upon by a force, and money moves. In the ancient past, the Egyptians and the Romans made an unsparing investments of time and resources to transport obelisks in their full glory, drifting several hundred tons of granite down the Nile River, or building special ships to cross the Mediterranean Sea. While the Egyptians quarried and moved stones in reverence of their sun god, the Romans moved the Egyptian relic to demonstrate their military might.

"Obelisks mined near the banks of the Nile traveled downriver to locations where they stood for millennia. Then they crossed the Mediterranean to the shores of Roman emperors as trophies of war. Forced movements. Trade routes. Power follows trade," reflects Olivier, as she considers footage of the undulating Atlantic Ocean that follows the scene of her studio in Rome. The ocean stands in for the physical and temporal distance between Europe and America, and between the end of her fellowship and the arrival—six months later—of the obelisk in Philadelphia. Just as the artist draws attention to the weight of emptiness while carving the obelisk shell on camera, she draws attention to the vastness of the ocean that connects as much as it divides the histories of the continents of Africa, North America, and Europe.

In the video, Olivier evokes American abolitionist Sojourner Truth as the crates are seen being delivered to and unpacked at ICA in January 2020. By quoting Truth, who abandoned her birthname because she wanted "nothing of Egypt" as a freed person,[5] Olivier surfaces the haunting undercurrent of the trans-Atlantic crossing and the abominable trade of enslaved humans that the ocean carried for three centuries. Truth conjured Egypt as the site of bondage of the chosen people from the oppressive kingdom in order to condemn the institution of slavery in the United States. Olivier, an Afro-Caribbean American, contemplates the way in which slavery as an economic, political institution has been justified and glorified in history. "There are two Egypts for us," she deliberates, "'Egypt the land of Hebrew bondage, Egypt—the Black Land, a magnificent African civilization, the realm of powerful rulers.' Which of the two Africas is in African-American? In African-Caribbean? Which Africa is ours?"[6] Olivier quips, "We think of [Cleopatra's] beauty but not of her slaves." Olivier's obelisk is a project of rendering history from both above and below: the rise and fall of Egypt and Rome, kings and queens and the enslaved. She also considers the more recent past: colonial expansion of Europe, its enterprise in human trafficking across the Atlantic, and its continuing legacies. Only in the fullest recounting of the complicated histories of oppression and the struggles against it, can we begin to parse the contradictory position of claiming both the inheritance of Egypt and allegiance to the Israelites.

Struggles with the demands of history and living symbols permeate Olivier's practice. "Is it possible to hold opposing ideas and realities in one hand?" posited the artist in an opinion piece in the *Washington Post* in response to controversy surrounding *Witness*

---

5   Olivier quotes Sojourner Truth from Margaret Malamud, *African Americans and the Classics: Antiquity, Abolition and Activism* (London: I. B. Tauris, 2016). Malamud references Harriet Beecher Stowe's article "Sojourner Truth, the Libyan Sibyl" from 4 April 1863 available at https://www.theatlantic.com/magazine/archive/1863/04/sojourner-truth-the-libyan-sibyl/308775/.
Stowe quotes Truth, "when I left the house of bondage, I left everything behind. I wasn't going to keep nothing of Egypt on me."

6   Within her narration, Olivier paraphrases the following: "These words made me think hard about the Africa in 'African American.' Was it the Africa of royals and great states or the Africa of disposable commoners? Which Africa was it that we claimed? There was not one Africa. There never had been." from Saidiya V. Hartman, *Lose Your Mother: A Journey Along the Atlantic Slave Route* (New York: Farrar, Straus and Giroux, 2007), 30.

(2018), her public installation at the University of Kentucky in Lexington.[7] More accurately, the controversy stemmed from the 1938 mural by Ann Rice O'Hanlon, which, in its celebration of local history, incorporates stereotyped figures of Black and Indigenous people, either in servitude or as aggressors. Prominently displayed in the university's Memorial Hall, the forty-by-eight-foot mural had in recent years drawn the ire and condemnation of students for its racist representations of people of color. Selected to create a new public art in response to O'Hanlon's vision of Kentucky history, Olivier presented an installation in the hall's domed ceiling that featured the same Black and Brown figures in the mural, but apotheosized in the gilded ceiling, liberated from the narrative of white settlement on Indigenous land. Students remained adamant that O'Hanlon's mural must go, and along with it, the context and the raison d'être for Olivier's work. The artist maintained, "Can we harness the tough questions [the two works] raise to wade into the pain, complexity and frightening histories of America, and consider the possibilities and resilience of Black and Brown people?"[8]

Olivier underscored that her work did not "magically dispel or absolve the University of Kentucky from embedded, institutional white supremacy or oppression," nor does it "neatly tie up the 'race problem.'" She declared, "The day I completed my response to the mural was the day the university's real work needed to begin."[9] This sentiment is consistent with the artist's oeuvre, including the obelisk sculpture. The real work on *Moving the Obelisk* began after Olivier made the cardboard structure, which prompted her interrogation as the maker of a symbol widely appropriated and reappropriated throughout history. What does a twenty-first century rendition of an

7   Karyn Olivier, "Removing an Offensive Mural from the University of Kentucky Isn't 'Racial Justice,'" *Washington Post,* July 6, 2020, https://www.washingtonpost.com/opinions/2020/07/06/removing-an-offensive-mural-university-kentucky-isnt-racial-justice/.

8   Ibid.

9   Ibid.

obelisk do in an art exhibition in Philadelphia? Her narration for the video is an attempt at an answer.

The video captures art handlers at ICA mending and erecting Olivier's obelisk under the artist's careful direction; the process involves further cuts that truncate the sculpture by three feet in order to make it fit, just barely, in the fifteen-foot-high gallery. Olivier recalls in the narration that in the 1876 Worlds Fair in Philadelphia, the entrance to the Egyptian Court was flanked by two towers that mimicked the obelisks that traditionally marked temple entrances. Nineteenth century America was not immune to Egyptomania then sweeping through much of Europe via world's fairs that provided convenient opportunities to recreate the pomp and glory of past civilizations.

Although not addressed by Olivier, one of the most prominent examples of America's infatuation with Egypt from this period is the Washington Monument in the US capital. Not a true obelisk, since it comprises many stones, the monument was built in two phases, 1848–1854 and 1876–1884, with the gap years attributed to difficulty in fundraising (money moves), the war economy, and the political instability of the American Civil War.[10] Although the unsightly, half-built structure stood forlorn for twenty-two years, the monument was eventually completed and celebrated as the towering symbol of *e pluribus unum* (out of many, one)—the nation's motto—in an inauguration speech by politician and philanthropist Robert Winthrop.[11] The rhetoric used by Winthrop played up the building process itself;

---

10   "History and Culture," Washington Monument, National Park Service, last updated August 26, 2019, https://www.nps.gov/wamo/learn/historyculture/index.htm.

11   Curran et al. quotes Winthrop at length in *Obelisk*, "America is certainly at liberty to present new models in art as well as government, or to improve upon old ones; and, as I ventured to suggest some years ago, our monument to Washington will be all the more significant and symbolic in embodying, as it does, the idea of our cherished motto, E PLURIBUS UNUM. That compact, consolidated structure, with its countless blocks, inside and outside, held firmly in position by their own weight and pressure, will be ever an instructive type of the National strength and grandeur which can only be secured by the union of 'many in one,'" 271.
Originally published in The Dedication of the Washington National Monument, with Orations by Hon. Robert C. Winthrop and Hon. John W. Daniel, (Washington: Order of Congress, 1885), 52–53.

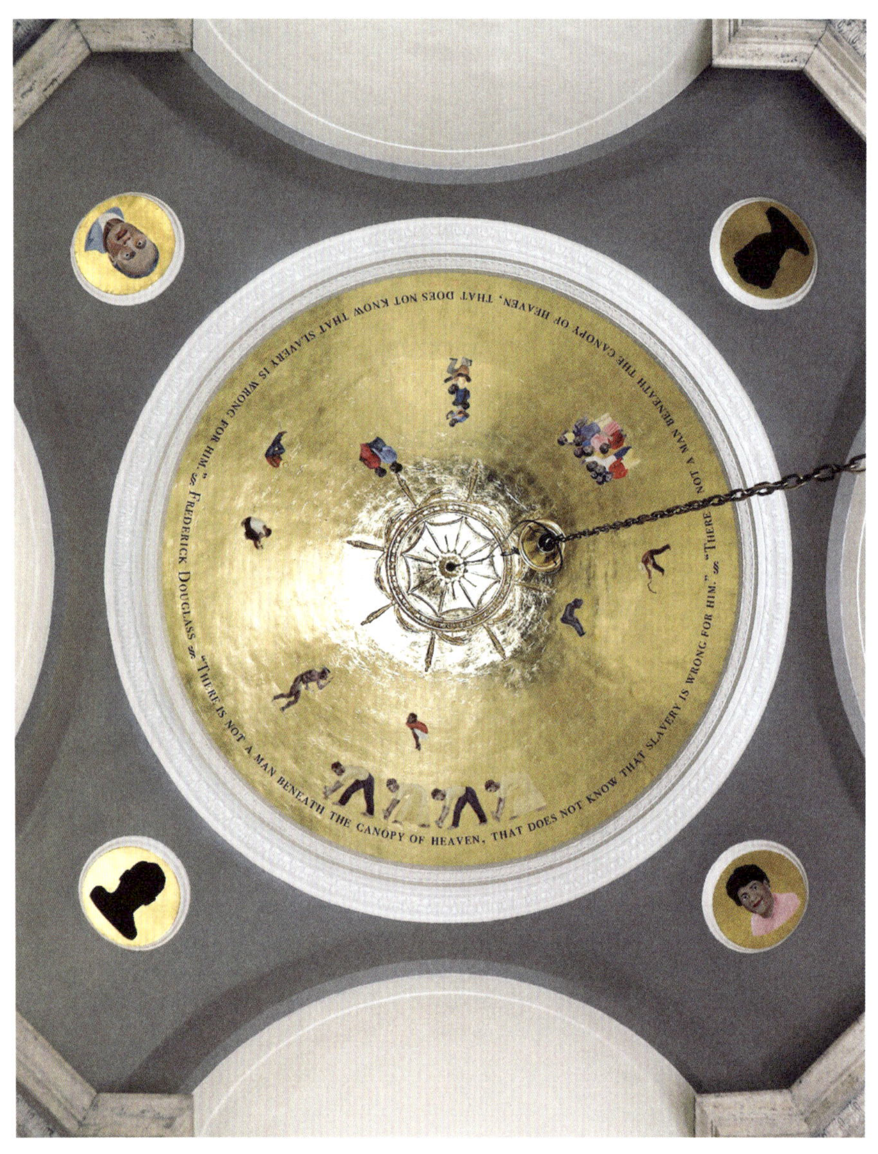

Witness, 2018
Memorial Hall, University of Kentucky, Lexington, Kentucky
Site-specific installation/commission
Gold leaf, paint and canvas
Courtesy of the artist

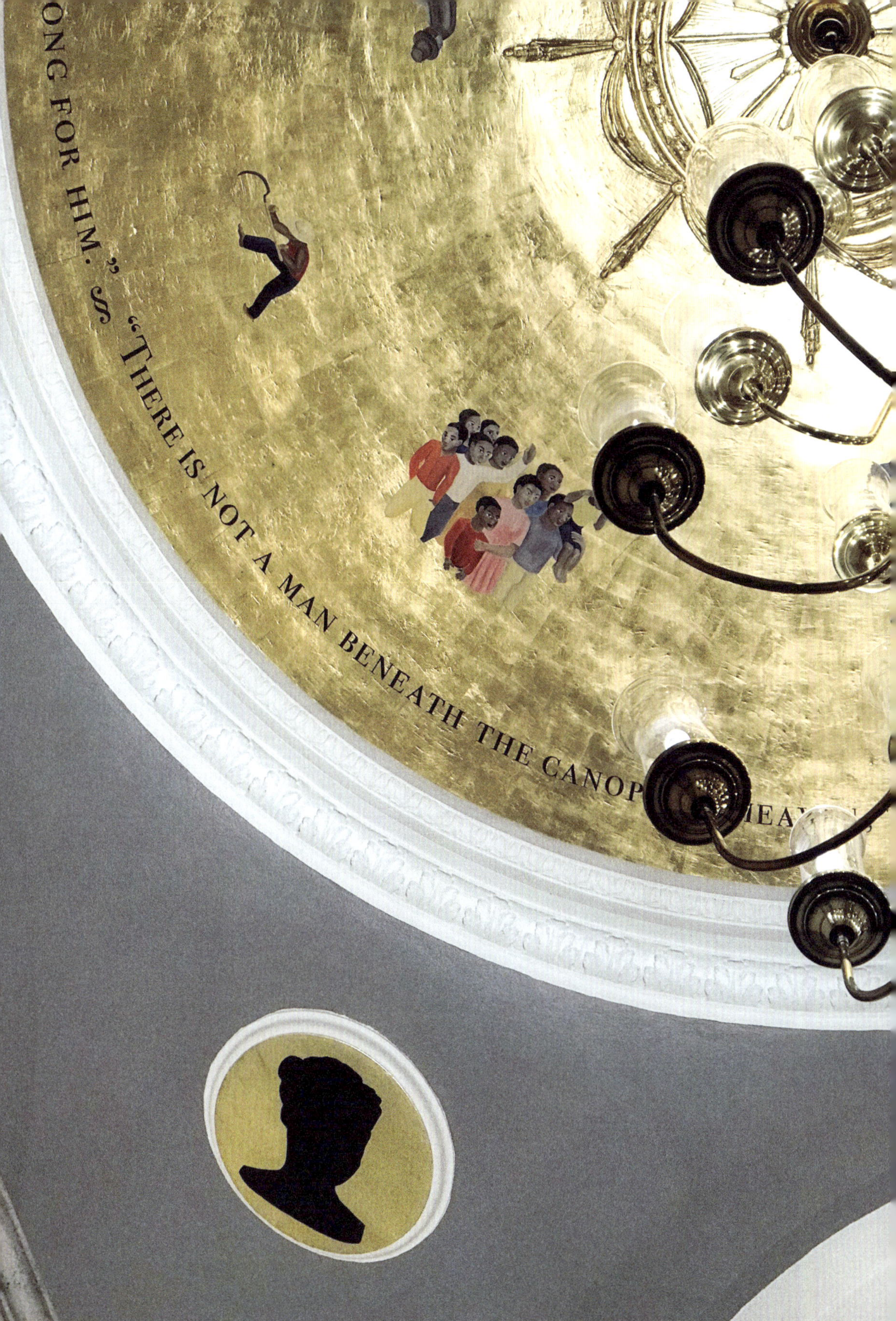
ONG FOR HIM."
"THERE IS NOT A MAN BENEATH THE CANOPY OF HEAVEN

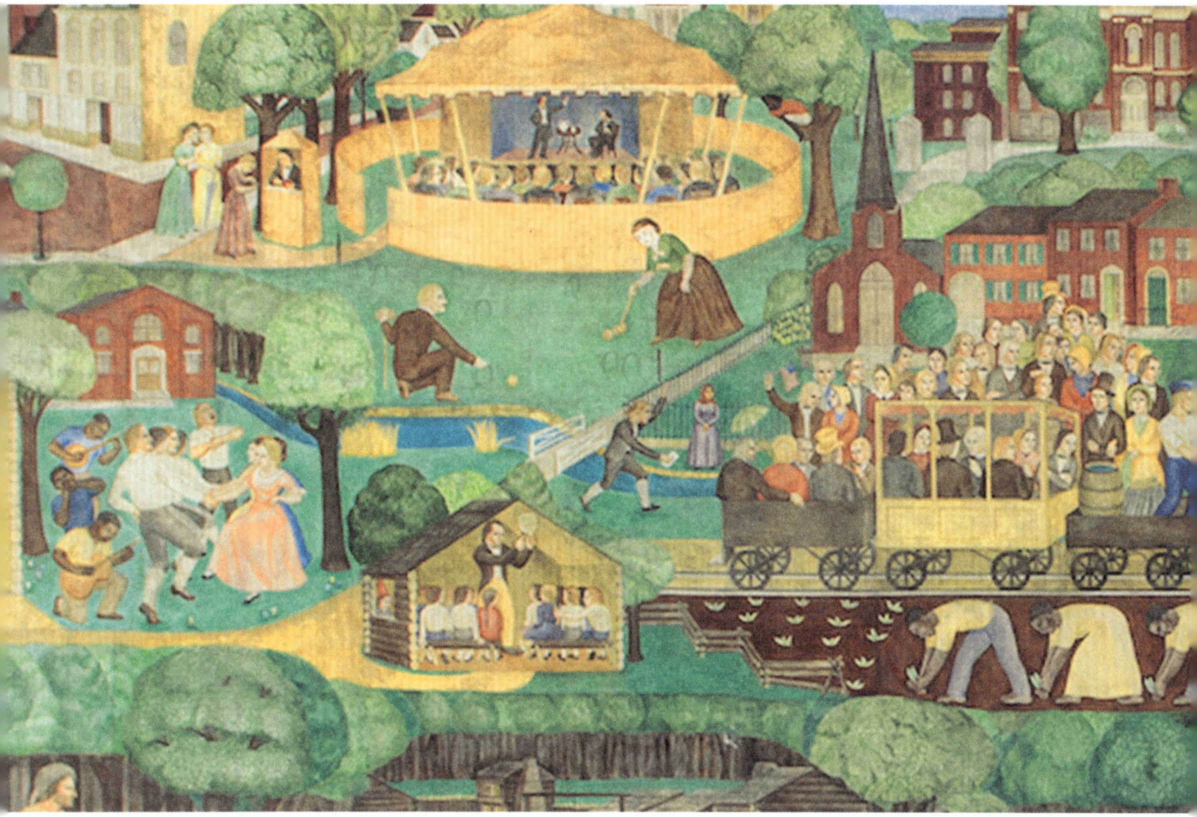

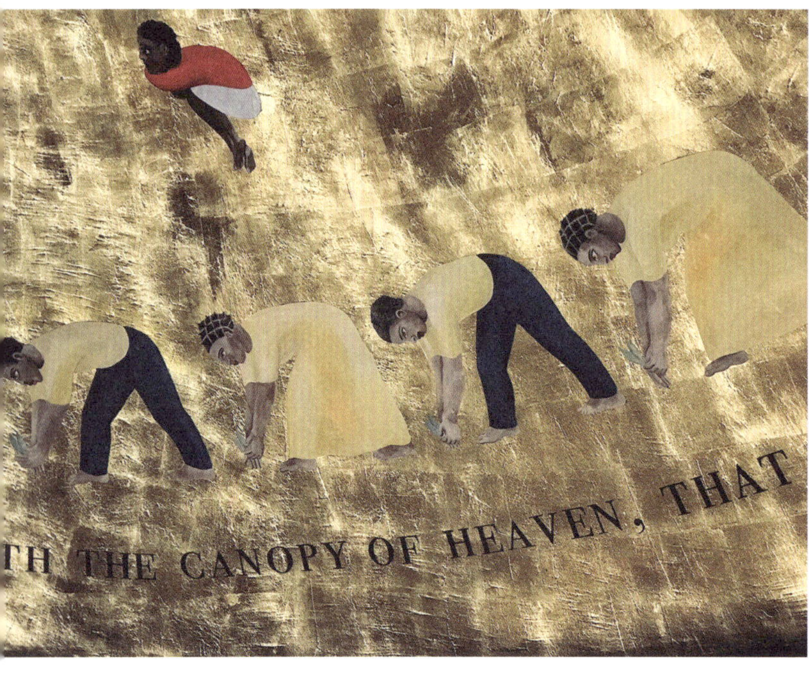
TH THE CANOPY OF HEAVEN, THAT

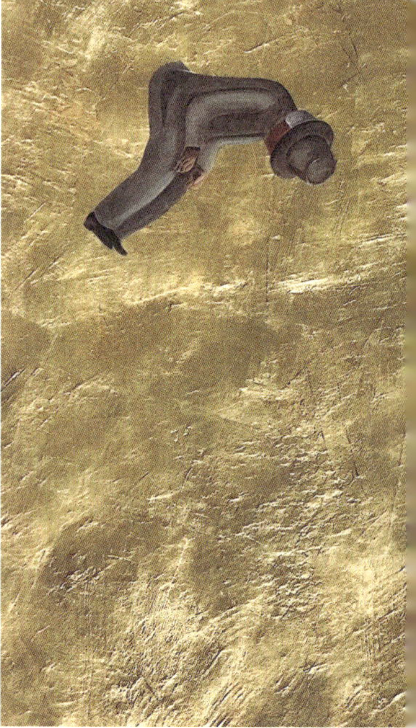

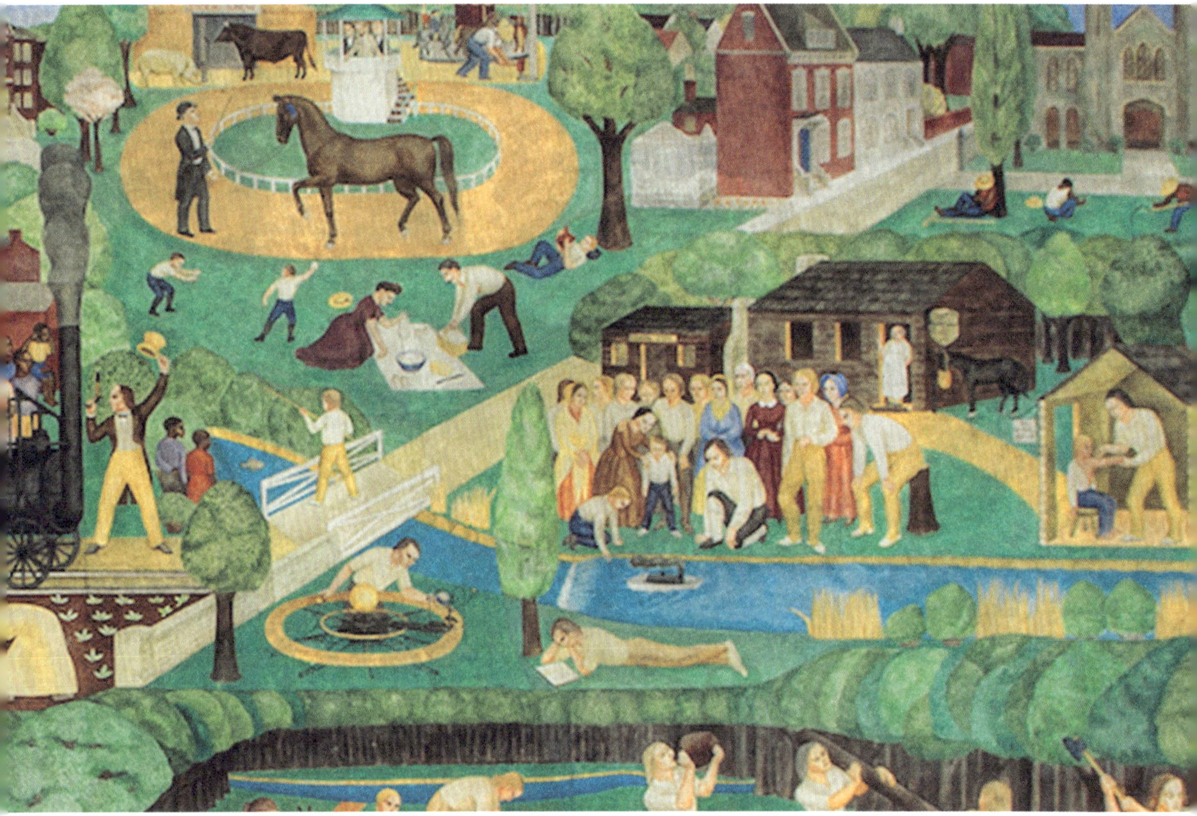

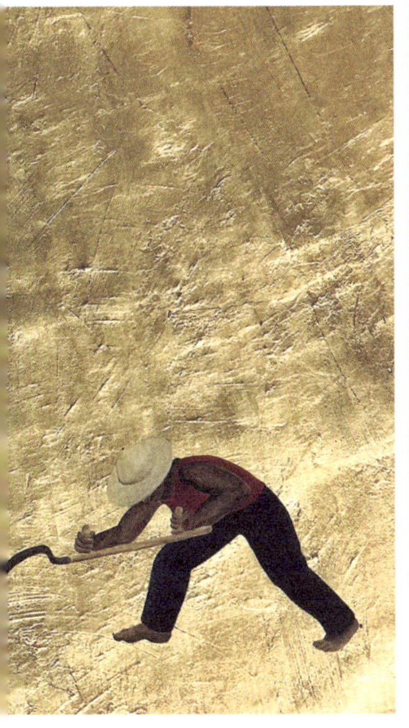
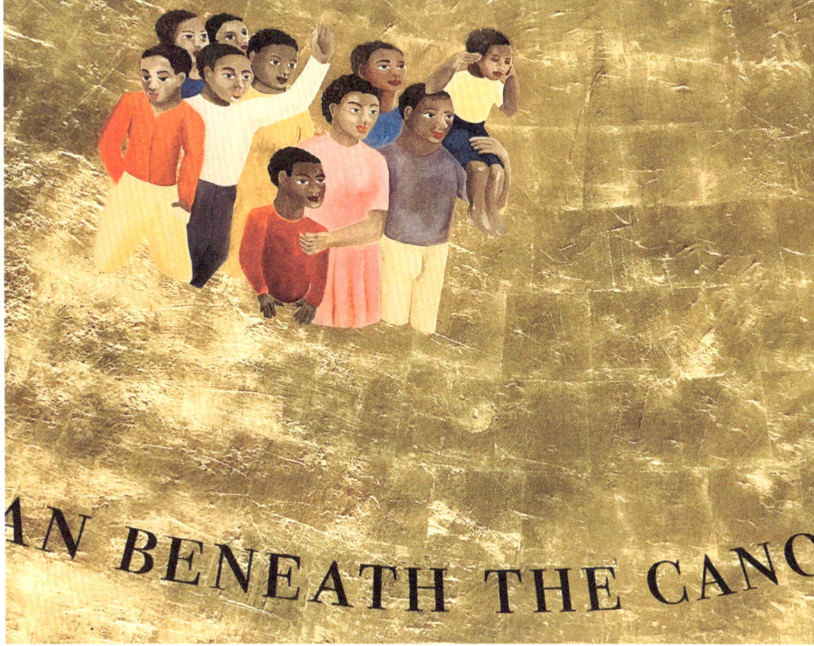
AN BENEATH THE CANO

rather than elevating a single stone that once stood for the monarchic power in ancient regimes, he claimed that the new republic's version of the obelisk saluted the collective strength of many individuals. This commendable reading of the monument notwithstanding, *e pluribus unum* as a sentiment of unity during Reconstruction masks the deeply entrenched political, racial, and class divides that continue to play out today. The national motto found new meaning in Olivier's exhibition at ICA, not only because the artist presented a crumbly earthen obelisk, but because an earlier work, *Fortified*, provided an alternate example of many becoming one; countless bricks comprise an imposing thirty-foot-long wall which, instead of conjuring a sense of optimistic unity, recalls the country's 45th president whose 2016 election promise was to build a wall between the US and Mexico to curb immigration. This, too, is part of American history and present reality—the xenophobia that has always accompanied the welcome of the huddled masses.

The Washington Monument is but one modern-day revision of the obelisk as a signifier of power, fit for the young nation. Recall Mussolini's monument, which drew its symbolic power from the connection to the Roman empire. Five years after the marble obelisk was erected, Mussolini commemorated Italy's invasion of Ethiopia by stealing an ancient stele from Axum (fourth century, CE), dubbed the Axum obelisk.[12] Again, technically not an obelisk given that it lacks a square base and pyramidion top, the stele was close enough in shape in the Italians' eyes. Especially after the humiliating defeat in the first Italo-Ethiopian war, Italy invested enormous resources on the triumphal showcase of this sacred relic in front of the Ministry for Italian Africa near Circus Maximus in Rome to demonstrate its superiority and legitimize its colonial rule in East Africa. While modern technology facilitated speedier transport, the Axum obelisk had to be

---

12   Curran et al., *Obelisk*, 291–293.
See also Angelo Del Boca, "The Myths, Suppressions, Denials, and Defaults of Italian Colonialism," in *A Place in the Sun: Africa in Italian Colonial Culture from Post-Unification to the Present*, ed. Patrizia Palumbo (Berkeley: University of California Press, 2003), 17–36.

cut into five sections and reassembled. Even when the stele was finally repatriated to Ethiopia in 2005, almost six decades after Italy was ordered to return it by a United Nations agreement in 1947, contemporary engineering could not spare it from once again being shipped in sections. The seventy-eight-foot pillar was returned in three parts on an Antonov An-124 aircraft, one segment at a time. In order to receive the largest, heaviest object ever to be transported by air, the airstrip in Axum required renovation and expansion. The cost of the return alone cost Italy $7.7 million.[13] The mending and re-erection of the obelisk followed three years later. These practical details, outrageously complicated as they are, become key parts of a long process of repatriation, the cost of which is both real and symbolic.

The logistics of moving Olivier's obelisk from Rome to Philadelphia paled in comparison to this leviathan project, yet the movement was motivated by a kindred spirit of repatriation. The Latin origin of *repatriation*, meaning literally to return to fatherland, is evident in the case of Axum obelisk; for Olivier, repatriation is not limited to taking back something stolen, but includes reclaiming history and its symbols, so that she may reconsider and reconstitute a form for new narratives and readings.

<hr>

13   "Obelisk Arrives Back in Ethiopia," *BBC*, April 19, 2005, http://news.bbc.co.uk/2/hi/africa/4458105.stm.

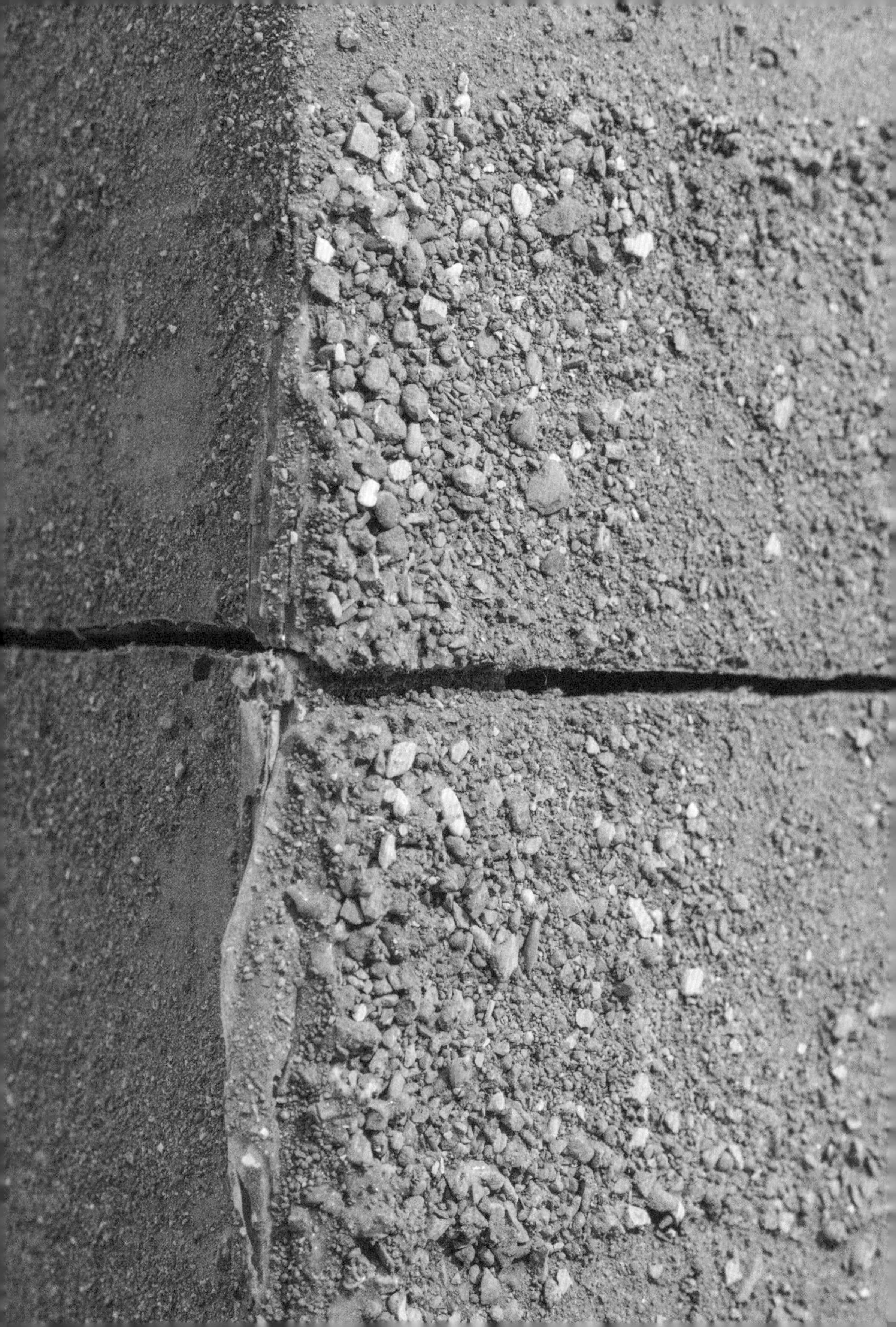

PART III:
EVERYTHING THAT'S ALIVE

The fistfuls of Roman dirt that Olivier applied like pigment to the cardboard surface of her obelisk were witness to history, just as the ocean was witness to its many crossings; the soil contains the evidence of many lives that once tread the earth. For those who have had to cross borders in search of refuge or a new home, soil represents a potential to take root. *Jus soli*—the right of soil in Latin or birthright citizenship—derives from a nativist ideology common in the Americas that acknowledges the reality of heightened migration in contradistinction to *jus sanguinis*—the right of blood or citizenship determined by the ethnicity or the nationality of parents. It can only be described as ironic that Italy holds steadfast to its *jus sanguinis* as a country that has as many registered immigrants within its borders as the number of registered Italians living abroad, with the greatest concentration in the US and Argentina, two countries that uphold birthright citizenship.[14] With the long-held American view on *jus soli* now challenged under the same president who promised to build the wall along its southern border to prevent immigration, soil as an artistic material holds metonymic power that exceeds national borders. Though capped by the gallery ceiling at ICA, Olivier's sculpture reaches skyward like all obelisks, connecting the celestial realm to the ground in Philadelphia in a symbolic transplanting of a piece of Rome.

At ICA, the obelisk is finally mended and re-erected, and its documentation completed and edited into a single video that accompanied the sculpture; video and the obelisk comprise *Moving the Obelisk* (2019–2020). Together, they invite the viewer into the artist's process, from the physical journey of crossing the Atlantic to the historical interrogation of the form that has been recycled by empire

---

14   For a discussion of transnational migration to and from Italy in light of the country's colonial legacy, see Teresa Fiore, *Pre-Occupied Spaces: Remapping Italy's Transnational Migrations and Colonial Legacies* (New York: Fordham UP, 2017). Fiore compares a 2013 statistic of 4,636,647 Italian citizens registered abroad to a 2014 statistic of 4,922,085 immigrants in Italy to make a point that the fear of an immigrant invasion is completely unfounded and even ironic based on Italy's own history of massive emigration.

after empire, to a final reflection on what it means to see a scarred cardboard obelisk in Philadelphia. This could have been the end of this essay, but the work does not stop here.

On March 11, 2020, the World Health Organization declared COVID-19 a pandemic and, along with practically all non-essential services, ICA prematurely closed Olivier's exhibition *Everything That's Alive Moves*.[15] The pandemic has disproportionately affected and claimed the lives of working class, Black and Brown people, as well as the elderly and immune-compromised. On May 25, 2020, a white police officer murdered a Black man named George Floyd in Minneapolis; as horrific as it was, the incident was but one in a string of criminal police misconduct and hate-filled attacks on Black people in the US. Smartphone video capturing Floyd's murder sparked nationwide and worldwide protests, and a grassroots movement under the banner of Black Lives Matter called to defund the police and dismantle white supremacy. Some of the protesters took to toppling monuments erected to glorify enslavers, war criminals, and genocidal colonialists. It was during this time, in July 2020, Olivier published her *Washington Post* opinion piece, not to defend the anachronistic depictions of people of color in the New Deal-era mural, but to defend her right to remember all aspects of American history: the painful, the violent, and the abominable.

It was also during this tumultuous summer that the obelisk arrived in Buffalo, where it was shown again as part of the tour of *Everything That's Alive Moves* at the University at Buffalo Art Galleries where I am Curator of Exhibitions. As I considered the significance of Olivier's exhibition in the border town of Buffalo and the historic stop of the Underground Railroad, I too witnessed and took part in peaceful protests against police brutality and racial profiling at Niagara Square, in front of the imposing thirty-two-story Art Deco City Hall. In the middle of the square stands a white marble obelisk, built and

15   "WHO Director-General's opening remarks at the media briefing on COVID-19,"
      World Health Organization, March 11, 2020, https://www.who.int/dg/speeches/detail/
      who-director-general-s-opening-remarks-at-the-media-briefing-on-covid-19---11-
      march-2020.

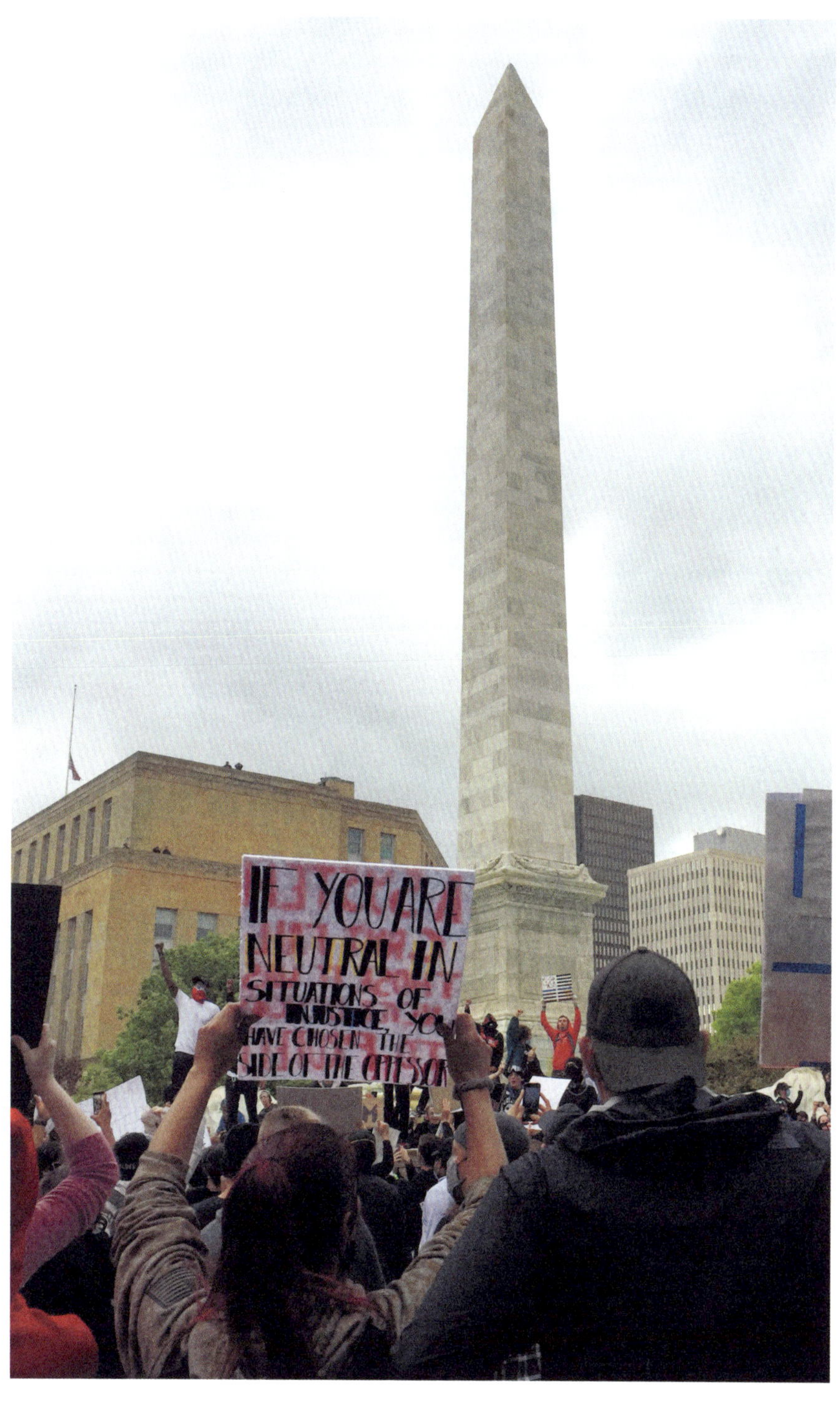

McKinley Monument, Niagara Square, Buffalo, NY, 2020

dedicated in 1907 to the former US president William McKinley, who was assassinated at the Pan-American Exposition in Buffalo in 1901. Technically, Niagara Square is a circular plot of land, and technically, the McKinley Monument is not a true obelisk since it is made from a mix of different marbles. But as history has shown with the Washington Monument and the Axum obelisk, such technicalities matter little when the symbol has a magnetic draw. For weeks during the summer of 2020, Black Lives Matter protesters and occupiers took over what was essentially a traffic circle in front of City Hall to lay claim to a symbol. There, I saw the red, green, and black African-American flag, designed by artist David Hammons, flown by the obelisk. It was also here that the Buffalo Police were caught on film shoving Martin Gugino, a seventy-five-year-old peace activist, to the ground, causing him a fractured skull and brain injury.[16] It is these acts of support and rejection of Black Lives Matter protests that connect the city of Buffalo to the historical narratives Olivier traces in *Moving the Obelisk*.

At the University at Buffalo Art Galleries, Olivier had to truncate her obelisk by an additional three feet to make it fit in our twelve-foot-high gallery. This time, the cut and the mending were not documented on film. When I asked Olivier what she planned to do with the cut pieces, she said she would keep them in the hope of presenting the work at its full height, its Frankenstein stitches visible in all their glory.

16   Jacqueline Rose and Eric Levenson, "Buffalo Protester Martin Gugino Has a Fractured Skull and Cannot Walk," *CNN*, June 16, 2020, https://www.cnn.com/2020/06/16/us/martin-gugino-protester-skull/index.html.

Karyn Olivier: The Golden Trophies

ANDRIANNA CAMPBELL-LAFLEUR

At ICA, we removed the walls in the space…[to continue exploring] issues I had addressed with the piece *Wall*. This new context [suggested] a different way in which a wall could be understood…the complicated ways in which territory could be [scrutinized]. *Fortified* was massive, and [required] five people [to work] on it. They were painters, [fellow] artists. [It felt] like a collaboration because so many people put their energies into it. [When I look to it, I feel the will and force of many, the power of our collective.][1]

Karyn Olivier

At ICA, Karyn Olivier installed *Fortified* (2020), which towered over the observer with hundreds of bricks, racked with clothes and stacked to the ceiling. The work operated at a macro level of fortification building and at a micro level of local clothing swaps, rumor mills, within the microhistories of the Philadelphia north end community.[2] As opposed to other dividing structures, Olivier encouraged staff, family, friends and neighbors willingly to donate personal

---

1   Karyn Olivier, Phone interview with author Andrianna Campbell-LaFleur, April 10, 2020. Oliver edited her quotes in February 2021. McKee noticed similar concerns in C. C. McKee, "Karyn Olivier, 'Institute of Contemporary Art, University of Pennsylvania,' *Artforum* (May/June 2020). Accessed May 2020 on https://www.artforum.com/print/reviews/202005/karyn-olivier-82858. Katy Donoghue, "Karyn Olivier: Thinking About Monuments, Memory and Absence" *Whitewall* (Summer 2020), 63.

2   The legacy of belligerent territorial grabs memorialized in Philadelphia is acknowledged in Olivier's installations. See Thomas Hine, "Art and Monuments at the ICA, Philly Sculptors Grapple with Who Gets Celebrated," *Philadelphia Inquirer*, February 16, 2020, https://www.inquirer.com/arts/university-of-pennsylvania-penn-ica-contemporary-art-review-20200216.html. For a discussion by artists such as Sharon Hayes and art historian Erika Doss on monuments and change, see Jon Spayde, "Monumental Changes: New Thinking about Historical Monuments Is Embracing Inclusivity and Ambiguity," *Public Art Review* 29 (57), https://forecastpublicart.org/monumental-changes.

objects to construct her temporary fortification.[3] *Fortified* also brings to mind the sculptural installations of Liam Gillick, an artist whose "negotiation spaces" replicated open office designs of the 1990s. Then corporate interior designers sought design solutions to entice people to congregate in the low-stakes "idea-hubs" that naturally occur in corporate hallways. Both artists rely on passers-by to animate large sculptures and monuments. Though relevant to today's conversation, most of Olivier's artwork at ICA was inspired by ancient Italy; she remembered: "For the past seven months I have been living in Rome, a city where monuments confront passer[s]by at every turn."[4] From these encounters, Olivier decided that at their crux, monuments are— psychological, physical, and cultural.[5] They may catalytically create a space of discourse.[6] These spaces may be informal, and yet congruent with the ways that democracy and dialogue function. In their physical manifestation, monuments are dialogues in the present about a time past. A consensual crossing of thresholds, where confrontation is desired, encouraged and acknowledged, this is the declarative maneuver that Olivier empowers. Mary Leclère, associate director of the Core Program at Museum of Fine Arts, Houston, described Olivier's 2003 installation *Fort* as a "thick-walled" structure that

---

3   This was not the first time Olivier involved the general public in the creation of her artwork. Discussing her 2010 performance and installation ACA Foods Free Library, Olivier described her performance at the Gwangju Biennial as similarly concerned with how viewers and participants "show up, act, give, create." See Claire Tancons, *The 7th Gwangju Biennial: Annual Report Gwangju Biennale*, (Gwangju, South Korea, 2008), np. See Nicholas Laughlin, "Hungry for Words" in *Rockstone and Bootheel: Contemporary West Indian Art*, edited by Kristina Newman-Scott and Yona Backer (Hartford: Real Art Ways, 2010) np. Olivier passed out carnations at the ICA opening. For a discussion of flowers, monuments and memorialization, listen to Ebony G. Patterson discussion of her work with flowers, clothes, bodily ornamentation and monuments on Tyler Green, "The Modern Art Notes Podcast" *No. 391 Monuments and Memorials*. (May 2, 2019). https://manpodcast.com/portfolio/no-391-monuments-and-memorials/. He interviewed three guests at the Pennsylvania Academy of the Fine Arts Professor Sarah Beetham, artist and activist Julia Pulawski, and artist Ebony G. Patterson.

4   Karyn Olivier, Phone interview with author Andrianna Campbell-LaFleur, April 10, 2020. Olivier has reiterated these statements since she began making these temporary monuments.

5   Ibid.

6   Ibid.

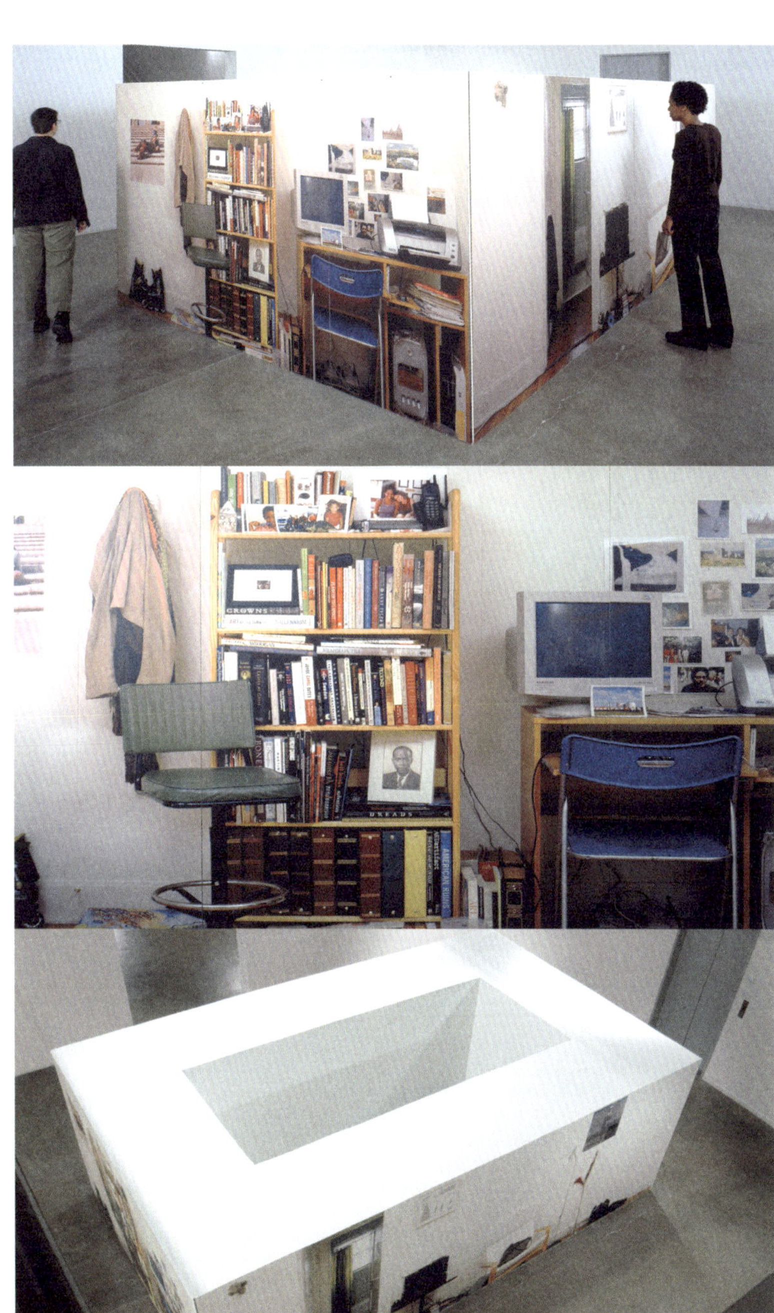

Above:
Fort, 2003
Installation. Photo of artist's living room
printed on sheetrock, sheetrock, metal
studs and paint. 18 × 6 × 11 ft.
Courtesy of the artist

p 132–135
Fortified, 2018–2020
Bricks, used clothing, and steel
Dimensions variable
Courtesy of the artist and Tanya Bonakdar
Gallery, New York / Los Angeles

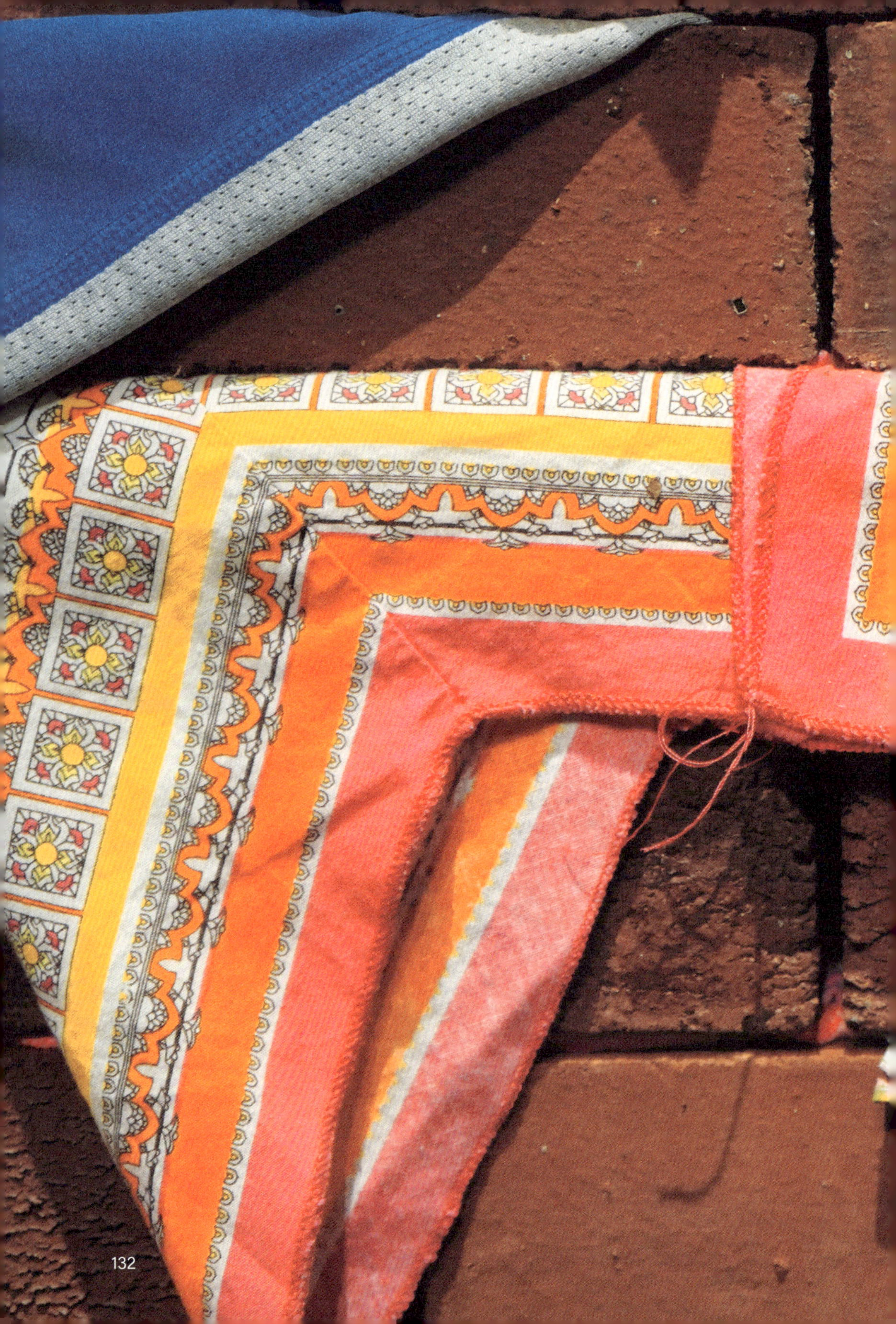

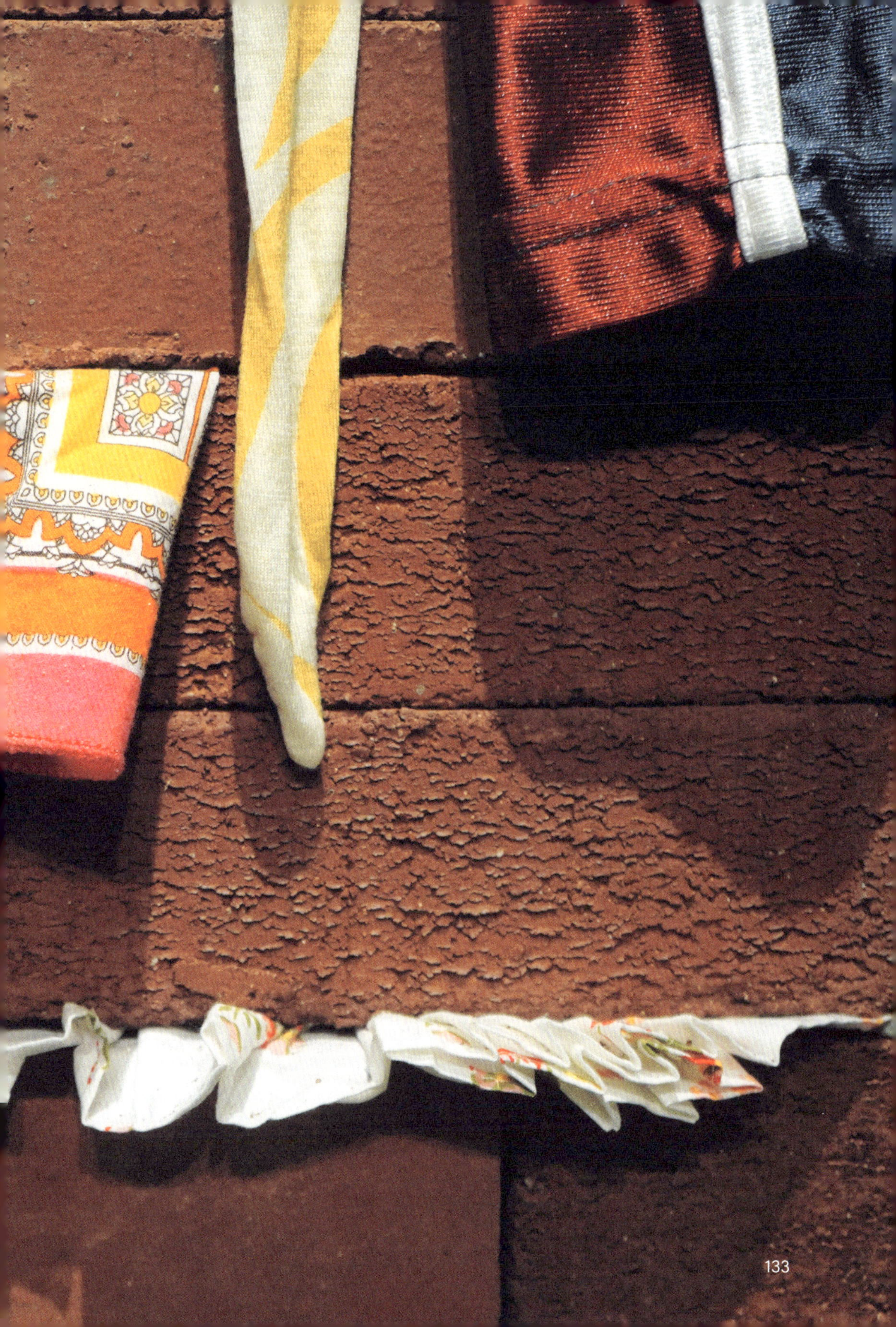

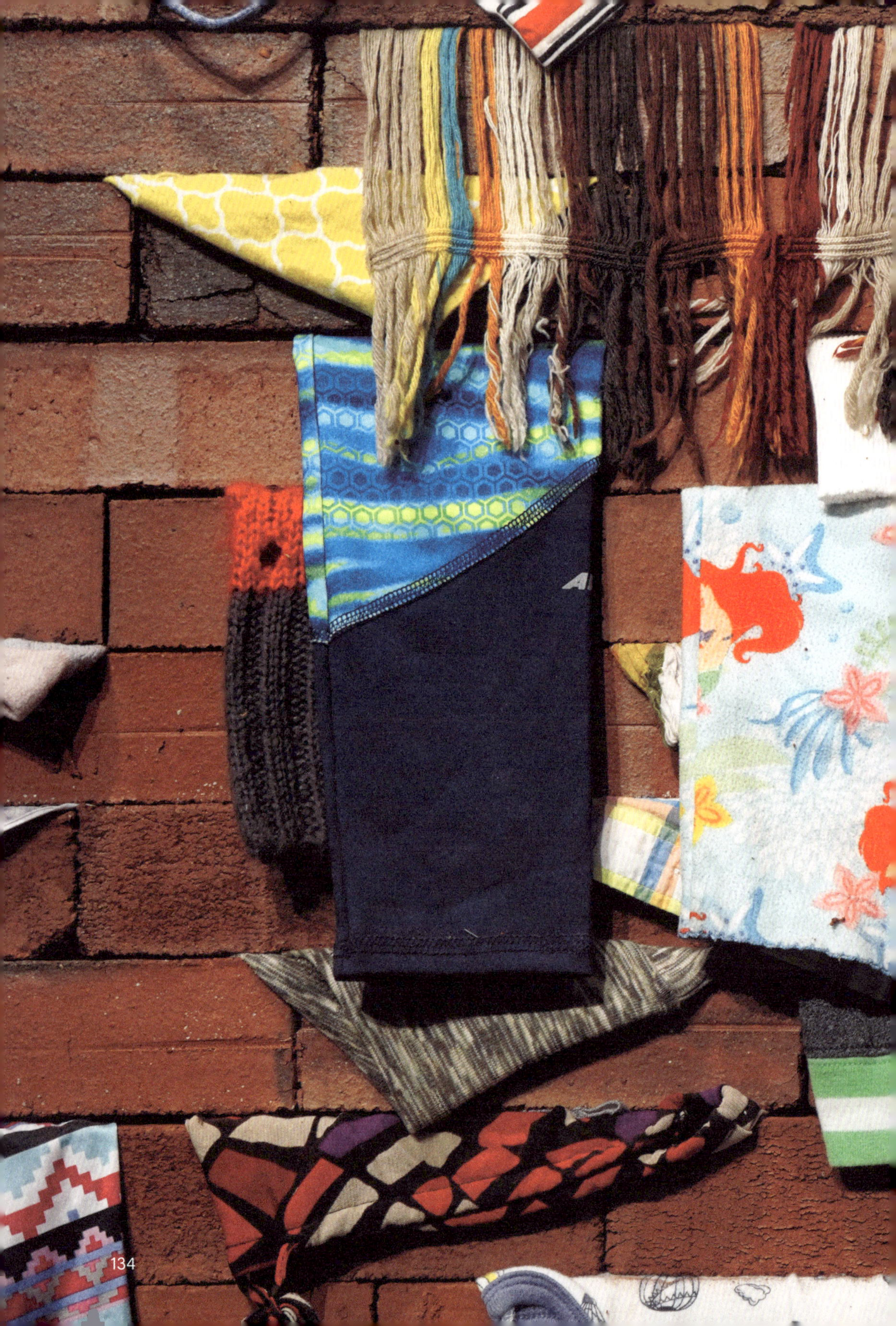

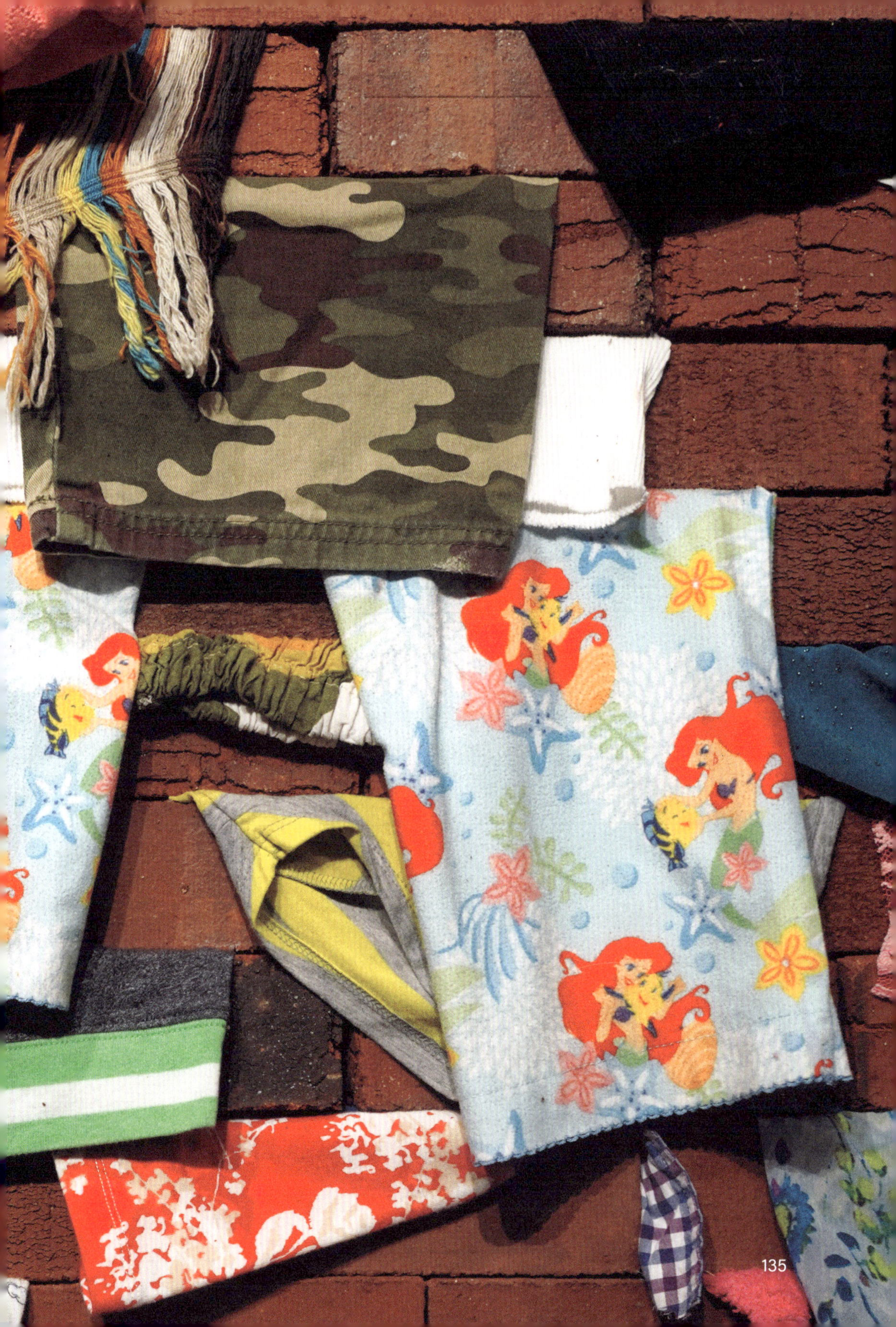

"essentially expand[ed] the Minimalist cube to architectural scale."[7] *Fortified* was a massive structure made of vertical steel beams placed every twenty-four inches perpendicularly intersecting twenty-inch-high metal lines. While in Rome, Olivier observed the 3rd century Aurelian wall, the largest extant border wall and that memory guided her to carefully lay bricks buttressing the improbably scaled wall of *Fortified* and to fasten the metal infrastructure together with unseen zip ties. In lieu of mortar, Olivier replaced traditional cement with saved clothing she collected from bundlers and donations by museum employees, family and friends:

> Staff from ICA gave me clothing. It was important that
> everything be used, worn. It was especially meaningful to
> have some items personally donated. It felt to me as though
> this made the piece unavoidably personal to the viewer.[8]

Clothing items, woven on looms with warp and weft, have a structural armature similar to walls; however, they are much more closely tailored and adjusted to the build of individual human bodies. Olivier suggests that clothing is an embodied surrogate. Curator Fitzgerald noticed Olivier's predilection for massing of bodily bulbous forms.[9] The non-descript, tawdry cheapness of the clothes, the faded blue jeans and shiny polyester shirts, evoke more of a dismal median than an idealized American normalcy.

---

7   Mary Leclère, "Spaces And (And As) Objects" in *Core 2003* exhibition (Houston: Glassell School of Art, Museum of Fine Arts, 2003), np. Valerie Cassel described Olivier's "Minimalist language," in *Black Light, White Noise: Sound and Light in Contemporary Art* (Houston: Contemporary Arts Museum, 2007), 54.

8   Karyn Olivier, Phone interview with author Andrianna Campbell-LaFleur, April 10, 2020.

9   Karyn Olivier, Phone interview with author Andrianna Campbell-LaFleur, April 10, 2020. Also discussed by Shannon Fitzgerald, she described the garments on as, "Transformed into a human proxy, the clothes pile creates an approachable dialogue with the viewer." See Shannon Fitzgerald, *Karyn Olivier: A Closer Look* (St. Louis: Laumeier Sculpture Park, 2007), np. Fitzgerald writes of the sculptures in terms of "discomfort and suggests eclipsed aspirations and diminished dreams."

Leclère observed that Olivier's installations are often site-specific and phenomenologically attuned to the conditions and measurements of the gallery space. This is true of *Fort* and *Fortified*. Olivier hybridized two modes of working that emerged in the 1960s: molding soft and hard construction materials such as Sam Gilliam, Jae Jarrell, Joe Overstreet, Franz Erhard Walther, and Claes Oldenburg did with their fabric objects and also assembling hard ready-made bricks as Mary Miss, Donald Judd and Carl Andre did in their oeuvre. Nevertheless, *Fortified* was not solely rooted in patterning 1960s methodologies. Soft-hard neo-minimalist interplay became popular in the installation art of the early 2000s, when artists such as Ethan Greenbaum assembled cylinder block walls and replaced grout with plasticine and acrylic medium. Notice thus, Olivier's brick installation was not a nostalgic gesture; rather her installation signaled a structural familiarity with contemporary art and in doing so referred back hundreds of years into the spatial politics of Philadelphia's brickscape. Her strategy—explored in this essay in the recent examples of *Fortified* and *Moving the Obelisk* (2019-2020)—began with basic structures that she rebuilt in order to reveal laudatory memorialization and the sometimes-subtle naturalization of abhorrent discrimination into the built environment.

The artist achieved soft eyes: a perspectival shift, a flip. By moving the wall inside, and chipping away its melancholic power, she constructed an environment that unsettled the power and hierarchy of monumental architecture. For the artist, the gallery experience contrasted with viewing local permanent monuments and artifacts in Philadelphia such as the Liberty Bell, a copy of the Declaration of Independence at the American Philosophical Society, and other objects that historicize and commemorate the founding of the United States. Immigration is a lens of sight that peppers the work. Born in Trinidad and Tobago, Olivier considers the legacies of colonialism in her installations and sculptural objects. Material choices such as clothing are frequently used to make motile totemic structures for masquerades and carnivals throughout the Caribbean and South America.

The viewer is also titularly made aware of this legacy. Olivier titled her sculpture *Moko Limbo* (2006) after the Moko Jumbies or "dancing spirits," who wear clothing and stilts.[10] *Moko Limbo* has some of the erect slender stature of Olivier's *Moving the Obelisk* in which she diminished the gigantic size and hard materiality of the monument into a paper structure. When Olivier resided in Italy during her Rome Prize Fellowship, she worked on the construction of *Moving the Obelisk*. The title referred to Olivier's transportation of the facsimile's passage from Rome to Philadelphia. The video that was streamable online and on view in the gallery allowed viewers to watch the packing and crating of the obelisk in her Rome studio and then the uncrating and erection of the obelisk. A team of artist assistants and art handlers (rather than the slaves that moved the original Egyptian obelisks to Rome) worked in unison to stand her structure.

Taken with the fact that Italy has more erect ancient obelisks than those in the African dynastic kingdom of Egypt, Olivier's decision to remake monumental artifacts in the gallery stemmed from her curiosity about the function of historical memory. Olivier was curious about the unique form. Obelisks are structurally imbricated with an Egyptian quality because they are believed to have originated in the Upper and Lower Delta of the Nile. Their subsequent absence from Egypt, the place of their origin, conveys how colonial histories are rampant with the erasure of the inventive creativity of people of color. As historian Molly Swetnam-Burland wrote about the ancient Egyptian obelisk that stands in the Piazza Montecitorio in Rome, "Even the Latin inscription visible today, proclaiming the annexation of Egypt, is in part reconstructed. In fact, despite the

---

10   Olivier's sculpture has been included in exhibitions focused on *Moko Jumbies* (Dancing Spirits) carnivals and Caribbeanity and these are the terms that she discussed her sculpture *Moko Limbo* 2006 (Paint, wood, foam: 8 × 12 × 6 inches). As do Sophie Sanders and Shervone Neckles in their catalogue introduction for the Tyler School of Art exhibition, where they explore the African influence on contemporary art. Sanders focused on, artwork that "share a common passion or perspective" and a "self-conscious response to censoring, impact, and celebration of Black and African Diaspora cultural aesthetics, which have been considered taboo in some historical contexts and iconic in others." Sophie Sanders, *From Taboo to Icon: The Africanist Turnabout* (Philadelphia: Crane Arts 2007) np.

intense interest of classical scholars in the Augustan monument, the monument is 'visible' to us only through the lens of its postantique history."[11] Swetnam-Burland points out, that too often we interpret obelisks within the context of Roman Augustan intrigue and Roman politics and thus aestheticize the Egyptian hieroglyphic narrative inscribed on the stones. There is no legible inscription on the hollow paper *Moving the Obelisk*. Only the shape of the sculpture, flat-sided and tapered, indicated its classification. Romans seized obelisks and carted them back to Rome during the Roman pact with Ptolemaic Egypt and continued after the annexation of Egypt in 30 CE. Because of the ubiquity of their Roman presence, anthropologists and historians focus on the Roman history of obelisks and continued to do so after ignoring their ontologies. This filters into the field of art history. In the past in conversation with colleagues, I questioned the ontological search for beginnings with regard to monuments, instead focusing on the hybridity and relation to fully immersed publics.[12] Nevertheless the foundations of a Western art history rests on narratives of innovation and this is problematic for cultures already maligned, othered, and ignored to not receive credit for their renaissances of generative creativity. Olivier's decision to recontextualize the obelisk at ICA counteracted that impulse of erasure commonplace in Western disciplines.

Olivier demonstrated that Western culture had a tendency to render even the plainly visible invisible. This art gesture was theorized by the architectural historian Robert Musil as early as 1927, nine years before he published his thoughts on the invisibility of

---

11   Molly Swetnam-Burland, "'Aegyptus Redacta': The Egyptian Obelisk in the Augustan Campus Martius" *The Art Bulletin* Vol. 92 No. 3 (September 2010): 139. Swetnam-Burland contravenes the case previously made for the lack of decipherability of the hieroglyphs in ancient Rome. For instance, Pliny the Elder's confusion of heights and attribution are excuses used to close an interpretation also based on ancient Egyptian historical context. Though this an article about ancient art, the remade obelisk traffics in narratives of the politics of power, piracy and plunder. See C. C. McKee, Karyn Olivier, "Institute of Contemporary Art, University of Pennsylvania," *Artforum* (May/June 2020). Accessed May 2020 on https://www.artforum.com/print/reviews/202005/karyn-olivier-82858.

12   See Andrianna Campbell, "Alphabet of the Revolution: Art & Activism in Cuba," *Frieze*, October 21, 2015, https://www.frieze.com/article/alphabet-the%C2%A0revolution.

the monument.[13] It is tempting to think of invisibility as the opposite of what is able to be seen. Invisibility—a malleable, patinaed blur—exists on a spectrum of possibility taking into account the unseen, the unrecognized, and the illegible. These distinctions also evoke questions of where power resides, and the ability of those who have puissance to laud, boast, disguise, contextualize, and garner acknowledgement.

We expect bureaucrats of the Roman Empire to obfuscate the lapidary originality in Egyptian precedent and to cherish obelisks as Roman golden trophies of war. In contrast, Olivier's impermanently-positioned obelisk has no hieroglyphs; it "has no content." Rather, the textured stone surface on cardboard is matte and smooth. She used the "shape-shifting" dirt to imbue the overall structure with a history that is more permanent than language. In the 1960s, following the dematerialization of the art object, participatory artistic practices flourished. Artists and scholars theorized that monuments could be visible, invisible, fluid, made and unmade by participating bodies.

Though Olivier made barricades, baileys, and other barriers for at least seventeen years, her artwork differs from other contemporary artists such as that of Sable Elyse Smith, an artist whose 2017 Queens Museum exhibition about prisons, barricades, walls, trauma, and surveillance interrogated the brutalities inherent to institutionalized constructed environments. Perhaps Olivier's experience in Rome heightened her desire to construct awe-inspiring fortifications and monuments. Her site in Philadelphia takes into account its contradictions: a city known for its masonry and bricklaying integral to nascent histories of colonial democracy, and also the site of anti-democratic actions by the state. For instance in interviews, Olivier discussed the 1985 bombing by the Philadelphia police that targeted the MOVE organization and the neighboring African-American

---

13   Robert Musil, "Monuments" in *Selected Writings*, Edited by Burton Pike,[originally published in German in 1936], (London& New York: Continuum 1998), 320.

community.[14] *Everything That's Alive Moves* should be interpreted not only as her response to the performative soft-sculpture of the 1960s, and as a return to the construction-site materials in installation art of the 2010s, but also as a big tent communal spirit.[15] After all, Olivier proclaimed that her work focused on art for varying publics. With her invitation to contribute clothing to *Fortified*, she led viewers to consider democracy as a safe act of the multiple (the masses) standardizing fittings for themselves, a general audience. Let us suppose that, quite wittily, Olivier interpreted this act of tailoring as the *demos* constructing their own democracies.[16] So that though Philadelphia's Federal and Colonial architectural monuments and cobblestone streets evoke the eighteenth and nineteenth centuries, their fixity contrasts with the adaptive nature of Olivier's use of cardboard and fabric materials. Both constructions evoke how we consider the gentle needs of the body politic. Olivier's work appears to be parallel and pertinent to the historical moment.

14   Anthony Elms, in conversation with Andrianna Campbell-LaFleur, ICA at the University of Pennsylvania, June 27, 2020. Elms's Zoom conversation with Karyn Olivier also references "dispersed monuments" and the MOVE bombing in west Philadelphia. See Elms, Anthony. Interviews Karyn Olivier. Zoom. May 20, 2020. See https://www.youtube.com/watch?time_continue=458&v=PEoTr5TFyBk&feature=emb_logo. The MOVE bombing has eerie crossovers with Honoré Daumier's print of massacre of families in Paris in 1834: *Rue Transnonain, Le 15 Avril 1834 [The Massacre at the Rue Transnonain, April 15. 1834]*.

15   Olivier's work is in a dialogue with contemporary artists rethinking the monument. Hank Willis Thomas has made t-shirts such as "ALL LI ES MATTER." Willis Thomas's collaboration with Eric Gottesman For Freedoms resulted in billboards across America. Judy Woodruff, Jeffrey Brown interviews Jane Golden about monumentality and the Monument Lab. Artists Hank Willis Thomas speaks about his Afro pick titled "Power to All People," Sharon Hayes on her plinths "If They Should Ask" and the 'Town Hall,' Karyn Olivier on her "The Battle is Joined," and Mel Chin's "Two Me". PBS NewsHour. https://www.pbs.org/newshour/show/philadelphia-public-art-project-ponders-meaning-behind-monuments. (October 9, 2017). Accessed July 10, 2020. Also see Olivier referenced in updating "contemporary resonance" of pre-existing monuments in Samantha Mitchell, "Philadelphia's Monument Lab Asks, 'What's Right for Public Space?'" (October 9, 2017) *Hyperallergic*. https://hyperallergic.com/404641/philadelphia-monument-lab/. Accessed July 10, 2020.

16   Claire Tancons, "Carnival and the Artistic Contract," *Nka Journal of Contemporary African Art* (Winter 2009), 117.

BIOGRAPHY

KARYN OLIVIER (born 1968, Trinidad and Tobago; lives Philadelphia) received her MFA at Cranbrook Academy of Art and her BA at Dartmouth College. In 2018 a permanent addendum was created by Olivier to a controversial Anne Rice O'Hanlon fresco in Lexington, Kentucky, calling attention to the African American and Native American figures within the piece. In 2015 she created a lenticular billboard in Central Park for Creative Time and a permanent sculpture for New York's Percent for Art Program. In 2019 Olivier was commissioned for the twenty-first-century Dinah Memorial at Stenton in Philadelphia. In 2022 Olivier will install a permanent memorial for Bethel Burying Ground, a nineteenth century African American cemetery. Olivier has exhibited at the Gwangju and Busan biennials, the World Festival of Black Arts and Culture (Dakar, Senegal), The Studio Museum in Harlem, The Whitney Museum of Art, MoMA P.S.1, The Museum of Fine Arts Houston, Contemporary Art Museum Houston, The Mattress Factory (Pittsburgh), SculptureCenter (New York), Drexel University, the University of the Arts, and the University of Delaware Museum, among others. She has received numerous awards, including the 2020 Anonymous Was a Woman Award, the 2018–2019 Nancy B. Negley Rome Prize, a John Simon Guggenheim Memorial Foundation Fellowship, the Joan Mitchell Foundation Award, the New York Foundation for the Arts Award, a Pollock-Krasner Foundation grant, the William H. Johnson Prize, the Louis Comfort Tiffany Foundation Biennial Award, a 2019 PEW Fellowship, a Creative Capital Foundation grant, and a Harpo Foundation grant. Olivier is associate professor of sculpture at Tyler School of Art and Architecture, Philadelphia.

CONTRIBUTORS

ANDRIANNA CAMPBELL-LAFLEUR received her PhD in Art History from the Graduate and University Center of the City University of New York in 2020. She specializes in art in the modern and contemporary period and her doctoral research focused on Norman Lewis and Abstract Expressionism. Alongside her scholarly research, she is the author of essays and reviews on contemporary art for *Artforum*, *Art in America*, and *Frieze*. In 2016, Campbell-LaFleur was a co-editor with Rachael Guynn Wilson and later Jonathan Patkowski of *Shift: A Graduate Journal of Visual and Material Culture*, and a special edition of the *International Review of African American Art* dedicated to Norman Lewis with Jacqueline Francis. She was a co-founding editor with Joanna Fiduccia of *apricota*, a journal of literary and contemporary art. She is the recipient of numerous fellowships and awards including the Dean K. Harrison Fellowship, the Preservation of American Modernists Award, the Library Fellowship from the American Philosophical Society, the Andrew W. Mellon Fellowship at the Dia Art Foundation, the Dissertation Writing Fellowship at the Schomburg Center, of the New York Public Library, and the CASVA Twelve-Month Chester Dale Fellowship from the National Gallery of Art for 2016–2017. In recent years, she has received writing residencies at the Robert Rauschenberg Foundation and the LeWitt/Mahler Foundation in Spoleto, IT. She has served as a board member for the Shandaken art residency and Paint School, as well as on the Art Advisory committees for the Civitella Ranieri Foundation and the Getty Art Research Institute.

ANTHONY ELMS is the Daniel and Brett Sundheim Chief Curator at Institute of Contemporary Art, University of Pennsylvania. With ICA, Elms has organized the exhibitions Milford Graves: *A Mind-Body Deal* (with Mark Christman, Artistic Director of Ars Nova Workshop), Cauleen Smith: *Give It or Leave It*, *Endless Shout*, Rodney McMillian: *The Black Show*, Christopher Knowles: *In a Word* (with writer Hilton Als), *White Petals Surround Your Yellow Heart*, and coordinated other projects. Elms's writings have appeared in many catalogs and edited collections, including a forthcoming collection of musician Arto Lindsay's lyrics. Essays, interviews, and reviews have also appeared in various periodicals, including *Afterall, Art Asia Pacific, ART PAPERS, Blank Forms, Cakewalk, East of Borneo, May Revue, Modern Painters,* and *New Art Examiner.* He has independently organized or co-curated many exhibitions, including: *Whitney Biennial 2014; Interstellar Low Ways* (with Huey Copeland); *A Unicorn Basking in the Light of Three Glowing Suns* (with Philip von Zweck); and *Sun Ra, El Saturn & Chicago's Afro-Futurist Underground, 1954–68* (with John Corbett and Terri Kapsalis).

LIZ PARK is Curator of Exhibitions at the University at Buffalo Art Galleries, the State University of New York. She was most recently the associate curator of the 2018 Carnegie International at Carnegie Museum of Art in Pittsburgh. She has curated exhibitions at a wide range of institutions including the Western Front, Vancouver; the Kitchen, New York; the Institute of Contemporary Art, University of Pennsylvania; the Miller Institute for Contemporary Art at Carnegie Mellon University, Pittsburgh; and Seoul Art Space_Geumcheon. Her writing has been published by *Afterall Online, Afterimage, ArtAsiaPacific, Performa Magazine, Fillip, Yishu: A Journal of Contemporary Chinese Art,* Pluto Press, and Ryerson University Press, among others. She was a Helena Rubinstein Fellow at the Whitney Independent Study Program in 2011–2012 and Whitney-Lauder Curatorial Fellow at ICA, in 2013–2015. Her research interests include mobility and migration as well as representations of violence in the colonial present.

ACKNOWLEDGMENTS

KARYN OLIVIER: EVERYTHING THAT'S ALIVE MOVES

Support for *Karyn Olivier: Everything That's Alive Moves* has been
provided by The Andy Warhol Foundation for the Visual Arts, the Edna
Wright Andrade Fund of the Philadelphia Foundation, the Henry Moore
Foundation, and by a Tyler Dean's Grant from Temple University.
Additional support has been provided by Nancy & Leonard Amoroso,
Danielle Mandelbaum Anderman, Cecile & Christopher D'Amelio, Cheri
& Steven Friedman, Christina Weiss Lurie, Josephine Magliocco, Lori
& John Reinsberg, Patricia & Howard Silverstein, and by Stephanie &
David Simon.

Institute of
Contemporary
University Art
of Pennsylvania

ICA is always Free. For All.
Free admission is courtesy of Amanda and Glenn Fuhrman.

ICA acknowledges the generous sponsorship of Barbara B. & Theodore
R. Aronson for exhibition publications. Programming at ICA has been
made possible in part by the Emily and Jerry Spiegel Fund to Support
Contemporary Culture and Visual Arts and the Lise Spiegel Wilks and
Jeffrey Wilks Family Foundation, and by Hilarie L. & Mitchell Morgan.
Marketing is supported by Pamela Toub Berkman & David J. Berkman,
and by Brett & Daniel Sundheim. Public Engagement is supported by the
Bernstein Public Engagement Fund. Exhibitions at ICA are supported
by Laura Tisch Broumand & Stafford Broumand, Catherine O'Connor
Carrafiell & John Carrafiell, Stacey Burke Frost & Benjamin Marc
Frost, Jennifer Otto-Klein & John Klein, and by Stephanie & David Simon.
Additional funding has been provided by The Horace W. Goldsmith
Foundation, ICA's Board of Advisors, friends and members of ICA, and
the University of Pennsylvania. General operating support is provided, in
part, by the Philadelphia Cultural Fund. ICA receives state arts funding
support through a grant from the Pennsylvania Council on the Arts, a
state agency funded by the Commonwealth of Pennsylvania and the
National Endowment for the Arts, a federal agency.

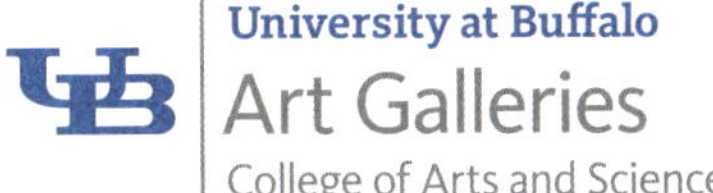

Support for the University at Buffalo Art Galleries is provided by the UB College of Arts and Sciences, the Visual Arts Building Fund, the UB Anderson Gallery Fund, and the Seymour H. Knox Foundation Fine Art Fund.

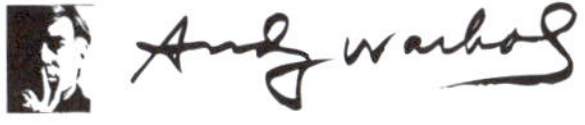

The Andy Warhol Foundation for the Visual Arts

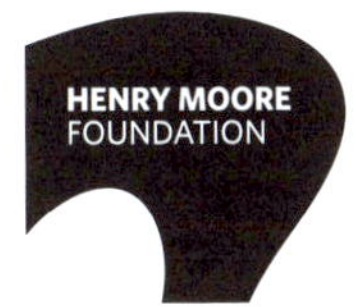

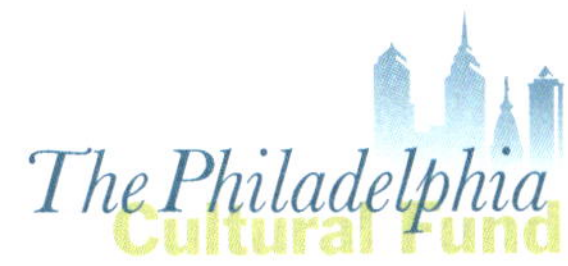

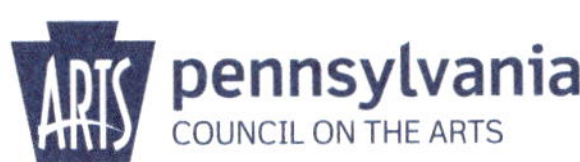

INSTITUTE OF CONTEMPORARY ART, UNIVERSITY OF PENNSYLVANIA

STAFF LIST (JANUARY–AUGUST 2020)

John McInerney, Interim Daniel W. Dietrich, II Director
Kate Abercrombie, Registrar
James E. Britt, Jr., DAJ Director of Public Engagement
Robert Chaney, Marc J. Leder Director of Curatorial Affairs
Elizabeth Chong, Visitor Services Coordinator
Lauren Downing, Executive Assistant to the Director
Anthony Elms, Daniel and Brett Sundheim Chief Curator
Shannon Freitas, Director of Administration
Taja Jones, Associate Director of Development & Alumni Relations
Jes Kaminski, Administrative Coordinator
Jill Katz, Director of Marketing & Communications
Daniella Rose King, Whitney-Lauder Curatorial Fellow
Alex Klein, Dorothy & Stephen R. Weber (CHE '60) Curator
Ali Abdel Mohsen, Digital Content Editor
Tausif Noor, Spiegel-Wilks Curatorial Fellow
Bruno Nouril, Director of Development & Alumni Relations
Meg Onli, Andrea B. Laporte Associate Curator
Caitlin Palmer, Curatorial Administrative Coordinator
Michele Pierson, Development Administrative Coordinator
Derek Rigby, Audio Visual Coordinator
Natalie Sandstrom, Programs Coordinator
Amanda Silberling, Van Doren Engagement Fellow
Paul Swenbeck, Chief Preparator & Building Administrator
Christina Yu, Assistant Director of Development & Alumni Relations

INSTALLATION CREW

Kat Bean
Dustin Campbell
Jacintha Clark
Jeremy Colonna
Hannah Declercq
Emily Elliott
Joy Feasley
David Harper

Will Harris
Jake Kehs
Adam Lovitz
Patrick Maguire
Drew Mitchell
Julia Policastro
Jay Roselius
Ash Williams

MOVING THE OBELISK

Itziar Bario, Camera
Ken Ard, Actor
Jacob Chris Hammes, Sound
Trapeta Mason, Narration

BOARD LIST

CHAIR
David E. Simon

VICE-CHAIRS
Bryan S. Verona
Lise Wilks

Danielle M. Anderman
Pamela Toub Berkman
Julie L. Bernstein
Charles X Block
Laura Tisch Broumand
Catherine Carrafiell
Jung Chai
Theodore Coons
Christopher J. D'Amelio
Benjamin M. Frost
Glenn Fuhrman
Andrea B. Laporte
Marc J. Leder
Michael Leja**
Josephine Magliocco
Hilarie L. Morgan
Midge G. Palley
Jennifer Otto-Klein
Lori W. Reinsberg
Allison Rubler
Katherine Sachs*
Ella B. Schaap*
Brett Sundheim
Stephen R. Weber
Caroline Gittis Werther
* Emerita
** Ex-officio

COLOPHON

This publication has been prepared in conjunction with *Karyn Olivier: Everything That's Alive Moves* organized by Anthony Elms, ICA Daniel and Brett Sundheim Chief Curator.
(January 24–Summer 2020)

Buffalo presentation organized by Liz Park, Curator of Exhibitions, UB Art Galleries
(October 29, 2020–May 15, 2021)

PUBLISHED BY:
Institute of Contemporary Art,
University of Pennsylvania
icaphila.org

All rights reserved. No part of this publication may be reproduced, stored in a retrieval system, or transmitted in any form or by any means, electronic, mechanical, photocopying, recording, or otherwise, without prior written permission from the publisher.

© 2021 Institute of Contemporary Art,
University of Pennsylvania

ISBN: 978 088454 153-0

EDITOR
Anthony Elms

COPYEDITOR
Gretchen Dykstra

DESIGN
Sonia Yoon

Printed in Italy.

PHOTO CREDITS
Video stills, p 10–30, p 109: Karyn Olivier; *Car Cover and Export Shoes* (detail), p 38–39: Karyn Olivier; *The Battle is Joined*, p 42–43: Karyn Olivier; *The Battle is Joined*, p 44–45: Steve Weinik; *It's Not Over 'Til It's Over*, p 52–53: Karyn Olivier; *Traffic Barricade With Fruit*, p 66–67: Karyn Olivier; *May 12, 1985*, p 70–71: Cally Iden; ICA, p 72–91: Constance Mensh; UB Art Galleries, p 92–99, p 122: Nando Alvarez-Perez; notebook, p 106–107: Karyn Olivier; Obelisk, p 111: Adam Eastland / Alamy Stock Photo; *Witness*, p 116–119: Karyn Olivier; McKinley Monument, p 125: Liz Park; *Fort*, p 131: Karyn Olivier; *Fortified*, p 132–135: Karyn Olivier; Endpages: Kait Privitera.

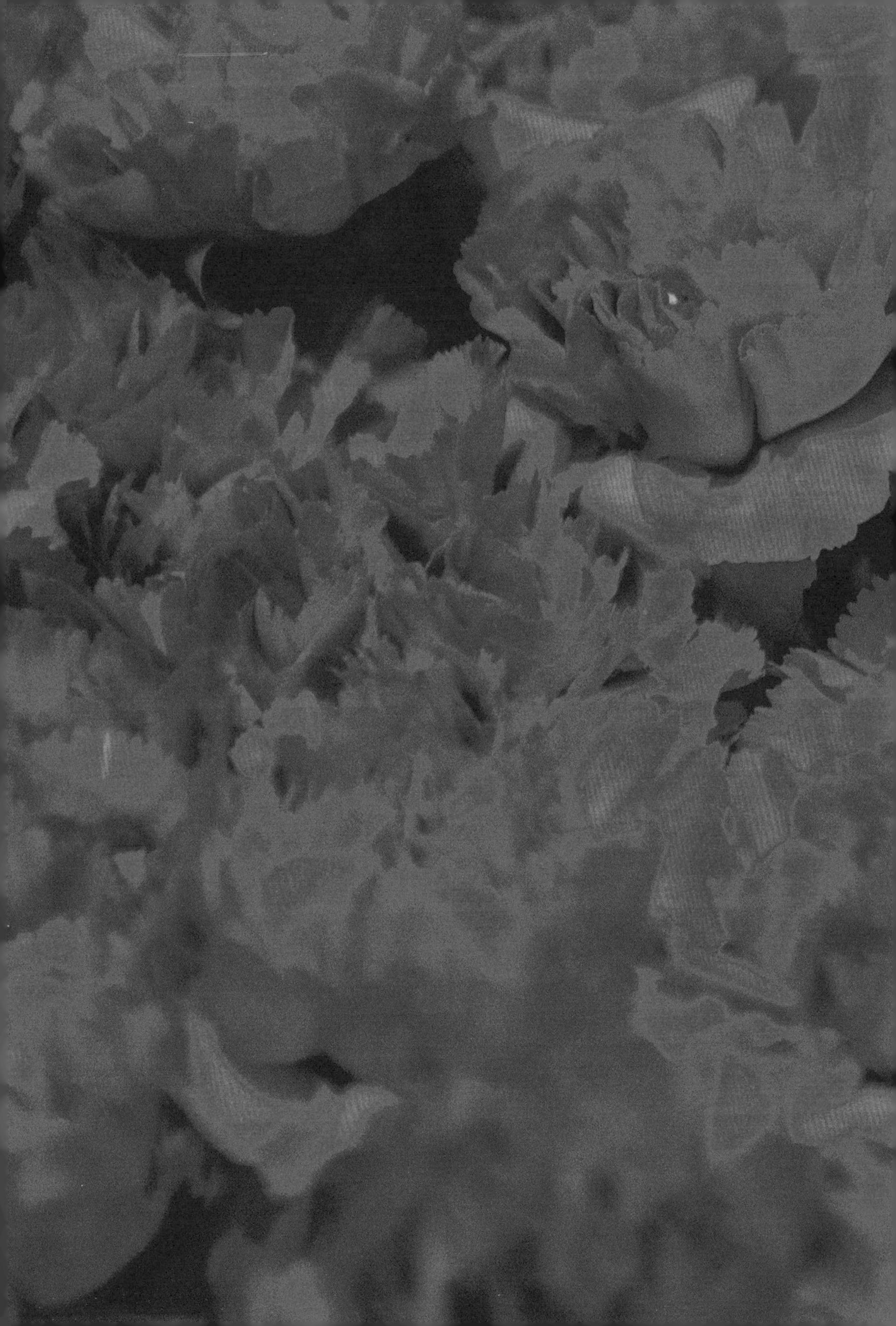